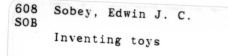

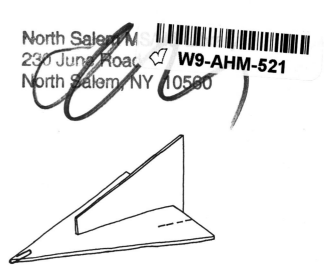

# Inventing Toys

# Inventing Toys

## Kids Having Fun Learning Science

ED SOBEY

# Zephyr Press

Tucson, Arizona

## About Zephyr Press

Founded in 1979 in Tucson, Arizona, Zephyr Press continually strives to provide quality, innovative products for our customers, with the goal of improving learning opportunities for all children. With a focus on gifted education, multiple intelligences, and brain-compatible learning, Zephyr Press material is selected to help *all* children reach their highest potential.

Inventing Toys: Kids Having Fun Learning Science

Grades 4–8

© 2002 by Ed Sobey

Printed in the United States of America

ISBN: 1-56976-124-8

Editing: Susan Kimber
Illustrations: Levi Miller, Crystal Karl
Design & Production: Dan Miedaner
Cover: Dan Miedaner

Published by:
Zephyr Press
P.O. Box 66006
Tucson, Arizona 85728-6006
800-232-2187
www.zephyrpress.com
www.i-home-school.com

Library of Congress Cataloging-in Publication Data

Sobey, Edwin J. C., 1948-
    Inventing toys : a hands-on discovery of science / Ed Sobey.
        p. cm.
    Includes bibliographical references.
    ISBN 1-56976-124-8 (alk. Paper)
        Inventions. 2. Children as inventors. 3. Learning by discovery. [1. Inventions.] I.
Title.

T339 .S695 2001
608—dc21                                                                          00-068587

# Contents

## Part III: Additional Activities and Resources

# Preface

One day when I was living in Akron, Ohio, I mentioned to our two sons that I was thinking of running an egg-drop contest at the National Invention Center (Inventure Place) there. I needed to get some idea of the types of devices kids would build to protect an egg from breaking when dropped from thirty feet up. Basically, I was recruiting our children to run experiments for me.

On my second trip to the grocery store to buy yet another dozen eggs it struck me that our sons were learning about physics, properties of materials, and experimental design. (I was learning to purchase eggs in quantity to avoid extra trips to the store.) The boys were having a blast doing science. At school, however, they were bored with science, which was taught in a traditional format with lots of lecture and a few cookbook labs. A subsequent visit to Science North, one of the best museums in North America, confirmed this: my children liked science but disliked science education.

My experiences during the decade since that time have confirmed in my mind that kids like science (as well as art, music, and other subjects) when they have the freedom to explore and express themselves. Unrestricted from conforming to someone else's learning style, pace, and interests, kids enjoy discovering and learning. Certainly the popularity of surfing the web supports that notion.

I developed this book as a tool to enable kids to experience doing science in the classroom. The workshops contained in the book have evolved as teachers and students from coast to coast experienced them and provided constructive criticism as well as enthusiastic feedback.

One fifth-grade student in the Tacoma Public Schools described her workshop as "the best day in school, ever." To get that kind of response, I will keep going to the grocery store to buy eggs or whatever else is needed. I hope you will, too.

# How to Use This Book

Inventing is unlike traditional schoolwork. It is creative, fast-paced, and student-directed. Students work in teams, share information and ideas, and help each other learn concepts and develop skills. To accommodate this style of learning, teachers need to restructure the classroom and classroom attitudes—and to a certain extent, they also have to restructure their own roles. This book was written to facilitate the process.

Part I of the book presents general information that will help the teacher to understand and structure the experience. This consists of theoretical and pedagogical background as well as practical information, including many tips drawn from the author's extensive experience conducting workshops for young inventors and their teachers. Topics presented in this section range from advice on how to structure the physical environment to general suggestions for assessment. Teachers should read Part I in its entirety before beginning the planning for their first workshop, and they may wish to refer to it at various times thereafter.

Part II, the core of the book, presents detailed teaching support for a series of six inventing workshops, each organized around a different challenge. Each workshop should take from 90 to 120 minutes to complete. Thus, when flexible scheduling is an option, it is possible to fit one workshop into a extended science teaching period. Alternatively, an enjoyable and efficient approach is to do several workshops in one day. This saves time rearranging the room, gathering tools and materials, and preparing students. Devoting a full day to inventing also makes a stronger impact on students and provides better reinforcement of the science concepts.

The workshops may be done in any order; however Workshop 1, Reverse Engineering, differs slightly from the others in focus. The challenge of this activity, rather than inventing a particular type of toy, is to use experimentation followed by direct observation as a means of verifying conjectures about how an existing toy works. Because this workshop builds analytical skills that will help students to improve their later inventions, it provides a good starting point for student inventors. (Note that this workshop can be conducted using two different types of widely available toy cars; an alternate set of workshop notes is provided to support the choice of either type of car.)

As part of the planning process for a workshop or workshops, the teacher should review the materials list, skim through the teaching notes, and look over the blackline masters that are provided for student handouts. Reviewing the Science Content and Teachable Moments sections just prior to conducting a workshop will make it easier to capitalize on the many opportunities for instruction that will arise during the course of the workshop. Correlations to American Association for the Advancement of Science Benchmarks and National Research Council Science Education Standards are also provided for each workshop.

Part III assembles various resources that the teacher may find helpful. These include a list of additional activities as well as sources for further information. Part III also contains the alternate version of Workshop 1, Reverse Engineering.

Aside from the instructions and directions provided, the overall guide to science and learning science is this: follow the most interesting path. This book can transport teachers and students to intellectual meadows from which dozens of trails originate. Following the one(s) that excite students will ensure that the class is on the right path.

# Part I

# Inventing to Learn

*Education is not the filling of a pail, but the lighting of a fire.*
—William Butler Yeats

# Inventing and Learning

## What is Inventing?

Inventing is the process of creating a new device or material, or a new variety of plant or animal. Although most people associate inventing with coming up with new ideas, ideas in themselves are not inventions. Inventing is really about making new things.

Until the inventor can prove a device works or a material can be made, it's not an invention. Most ideas for new products fail because no one takes them far enough to build a working model. Everyone has ideas, but only a few people take action on their ideas. Those who do, we label inventors.

The process of transforming the idea or the design into a working model is where the hard work of inventing (or creating) lies. Edison said that inventing is 1 percent inspiration and 99 percent perspiration. The hard work occurs as inventors encounter and solve problems no one can anticipate.

*As inventors transform ideas into working models, learning occurs.*

As inventors transform ideas into working models, learning occurs. Inventors have to learn how to use tools, materials, and processes that may be new to them. They have to do things that they have never done—and possibly no one else has. This requires experimentation: designing, building, conducting tests, collecting and interpreting data, and making changes—hopefully improvements—to their inventions.

Faced with limits imposed by nature and technology, inventors develop an understanding of science and engineering principles, and by necessity they are also exposed to marketing and business planning principles. Inventors, like scientists, writers, and artists, are lifelong learners. They learn because they need to learn to keep inventing—learning empowers them to do what they enjoy doing. This observation applies to education as well. By creating environments in which students become inventors, we help them to be more enthusiastic learners.

## Learning and Enjoyment

Professor Mihaly Csikszentmihalyi of the University of Chicago has studied inventors and other creative people. His research started with trying to understand why people enjoy some activities. In his book *Flow—The Psychology of Optimal Experience,* he lays out the handful of conditions that make a task or activity enjoyable:

1. The task, although possibly difficult to accomplish, is doable.
2. It is possible to concentrate on the task. Distractions can be eliminated.
3. The task has clear goals.
4. There is immediate feedback on progress.
5. The task consumes one's consciousness.
6. The worker has a sense of control over what he or she is doing.
7. Time passes quickly; one loses a sense of time.

Inventing and inventing to learn meet these conditions. Changing the learning process from a traditional flow of information to a challenging and thought-provoking activity where each learner injects his or her own creativity to help determine the outcome assures that the experience will be more enjoyable and learners will spend more time and effort on the learning tasks.

Inventing is not unique among creative pursuits in its association with learning and enjoyment. However, it is ideal for helping young students to learn science and technology as well as other subjects that can be woven into science projects.

## Benefits of Using Inventing to Promote Learning

There are two main benefits of using inventing as a pedagogic tool to enhance learning. First, inventing makes kids think. We know that students aren't just empty 2-liter bottles waiting to be filled with the great information we want to pour in. To get them to learn, we need them to make mental connections—we can't do that for them. To make mental connections they must think, and inventing forces this to happen.

Like all inventors, they will think because they encounter challenges they need to solve in order to make their inventions work. When students become inventors they thirst for the information and skills that will help them improve their inventions. As a matter of course, they will encounter and learn physics, investigative techniques, and engineering principles.

*Inventors, like scientists, writers, and artists, are lifelong learners.*

The second benefit is that students will eagerly spend time on the task. It is generally agreed that the longer students spend actively working and thinking about something, the more they will learn. Inventing gets kids to spend longer on tasks because the activity is fun (it matches the conditions found by Csikszentmihalyi) and because they are working on their own creations. They have ownership and responsibility for the completed project, and they learn enthusiastically.

Inventing has additional learning benefits as well. Among other things, it helps students to learn the skills most sought by employers: working cooperatively with others, solving problems, using materials and time wisely, acquiring and using information, and using tools (U.S. Department of Labor, 1991). Thus, inventing not only helps students to learn science content and research skills, it also helps prepare them for employment.

## Inventing versus Other Inquiry-Based Learning Approaches

How is inventing to learn different? In some inquiry-based learning, it is the author's or the teacher's questions that are investigated, not the student's. For example, in most lab experiences, students don't control the process, they follow the cookbook. There is one correct answer and, frankly, most kids don't care what it is—they just need an answer to write on their lab handouts. In such situations, creativity is rarely encouraged.

With inventing to learn, we give students the goals and general parameters of an activity, and then leave it up to them to figure out how to meet those goals through the process of creating and improving their own inventions. Instead of stifling their creativity because it interferes with the lesson plan, we encourage it.

Creativity is an extremely strong force—creative people will tell you that they complete their projects because they are driven to see them finished. If they need to learn a new skill or acquire new knowledge in order to finish, they will do so. Letting your students be creative in a directed way will unleash this powerful force to help them learn.

Building a class of creative learners does require giving them support when they try something new. They need to be able to experiment without fear of failure or ridicule. But the rewards are great: the more self-confident they become, the more creative they become, and the more creative they become, the more responsible they will be for their own learning.

# Structuring the Experience
## Getting Students Involved

From the moment students enter the classroom for an inventing workshop they should be engaged in the process of inventing to learn. Have a simple preworkshop warm-up activity ready, one that you can describe in a few words. The goals should be clear and the materials close at hand. Have students work in teams of two or three so everyone participates. Here are a few suggestions:

- **Straw structures.** Teams construct a tower as tall as possible using only straws and masking tape. Measure completed structures with a yardstick or meter stick.
- **Straw bridges.** Teams build a bridge to span the space between two adjacent tables, and see how much weight the bridge can hold. (Use some common material for weight, like a chalkboard eraser.)
- **Straw accessories.** Teams pick an action figure or doll and build an accessory that could be sold along with that toy.
- **Paper airplanes.** Teams make paper airplanes that fly into a narrow target (such as a Hula-Hoop® or open trash bag) from across the room.
- **New sandbox toy.** Teams design on paper a new toy that preschoolers could use in a sandbox or at the beach. If the requisite materials are available, have them build a model.

As teams work, wander around asking what they are doing and making positive comments on their designs and their progress. Show off creative designs to everyone to inspire their creativity.

At the outset or at an appropriate point in the activity, it is a good idea to announce difficult time limits for completion. This will establish a precedent for inventing workshops to come. Although every team won't be able to complete their project to the degree that they want, it's important for students to learn that during the learning stage of the inventing process it is not necessarily appropriate to perfect a design. Point out that inventors have to work quickly and "make mistakes as fast as possible" so they can learn.

---

## TiP

### Transform the Classroom

Students should recognize from the outset that a toy inventing workshop is different from what they are used to at school. To set the stage, try decorating the room. Drape yellow caution tape (available at hardware stores) around the perimeter and place signs outside and inside. Here are some suggestions:

- ✔ Inventors' Entrance
- ✔ (School name) Toy Design Laboratory
- ✔ Inventors ask questions.
- ✔ Collect creative ideas.
- ✔ Mistakes lead to understanding.
- ✔ Caution! Inventors At Work
- ✔ Great ideas start here.

Rearrange desks to facilitate work by groups of two or three students, and pull chairs aside, as students will be standing or moving throughout much of the workshop. Many of the activities require a large open space or an outside staging area for testing, so check the notes and prepare in advance.

Conclude the activity by having each team hold up their design solution and describe it. You can point out interesting features and compliment each team on some aspect of their work. Lead the class in applause for each team after they have finished presenting their ideas.

Now you have set the tenor for the day. You have emphasized that time is in critically short supply, that it is okay to make mistakes, that people have to work in teams and cooperate, and that we value the ideas of other people. You also have demonstrated that you expect each team to be accountable for its work and that each will show what they accomplished at the end of an activity.

## Issuing a Challenge

In an inventing workshop, the best way to lay out what you want students to do is to present it as a challenge. By issuing a challenge you establish that the students will take responsibility for the inventing and that they will have freedom to design and produce solutions of their own choosing. You also establish what the criteria are for evaluating success so everyone is aiming for the same target and can self-evaluate their progress.

Students will rise to the challenge provided that it sounds like fun and is something they think they can accomplish. Since people think of toys as being fun and since everyone has some expertise using them, toys are an ideal medium for physical inquiry.

When you issue the challenge, include a measurable goal. This focuses the activity and also makes it more enjoyable: shooting a squirt gun without a target quickly becomes boring, but when you add a target, especially a moving target, the exercise becomes much more fun.

The best goals are ones that require students to measure their success, record and graph the data, and interpret the results. Activities that meet these criteria help students learn not only the content, but also the processes of science.

### Reinvent Yourself

Before a toy inventing workshop, take a moment to visualize a new role for yourself—let go of your traditional teacher self and become a factory boss or the head of a design firm. Your goal is to manage the design and testing process so that it is safe and your workers make the most progress inventing and learning. Your new "job requirements" are:

✔ to create an atmosphere that is conducive to creativity and cooperation;

✔ to stimulate thinking by issuing challenges for students to meet;

✔ to encourage extended work by carefully criticizing, questioning, and offering open-ended suggestions.

Goals also encourage students to improve their inventions and learn as they do. Teams use numerical evaluations of goals as scores, and they want to improve their scores each time. Being able to measure their own progress—immediate feedback—means they are free to work on their own.

## Allowing Students to Work Freely

Letting the inventors pick their own way to meet the challenge is how ownership of the responsibility transfers from you to them. If you tell them how to solve the problem, any lack of success is your problem: "You told us to do it this way and it didn't work."

However, many students will need help getting started—ask students to invent a toy and they are likely to give you blank stares in return. Showing them a model will jump-start their creative process and launch them into the activity. A proven model will speed things up by preventing mistakes that don't contribute to the desired learning. However, once they have mastered the basic design, encourage students to be creative with additions, deletions, and other changes.

For example, students building pneumatic-blast rockets could spend countless unproductive hours trying to figure out how to make a rocket made of paper fly across a gym. By showing them how to make the fuselage of the rocket you speed up the process and let them focus on the more interesting aspects of controlling the flight with fins, nose cones, and weights.

### Use Inventor's Logs

Having students record their ideas and document their progress on paper will help them to get maximum learning value from an inventing workshop. Keeping an Inventor's Log is a convenient way for them to do this. However, if they start out by working in only two dimensions, many students won't be able to conceptualize how to design a mock-up, so you might want to let them work with actual materials first. Make sure they draw their designs later. They should also record data, details of experiments, and other information. In addition to the workshop-specific logs provided in Part II of the book, a generic log is provided at the end of this section. Alternatively, you may wish to design your own log to meet special needs of your students or specific assessment requirements.

Once started, teams and individuals need to have the freedom to fail. This is essential to the creative process, as mistakes are often more helpful to the learning process than successes are. It is therefore important not to stifle any ideas as long as they are serious. Don't allow students to ridicule creative disasters. Extol the ideas and talk about why the design didn't work. Congratulate the *team* for their creativity and industry, and analyze the *design* for its strengths and limitations.

## Expect a Little Noise

Considerable learning occurs between students and between groups. They share information, experience, and knowledge easily and will help each other understand the science behind the project. Thus the inventing classroom will be a noisy one with many discussions occurring simultaneously and continuously! You may want to establish rules for ending conversations when you need to talk to the class as a whole.

## Keep Everyone Engaged in Learning

When some teams succeed at a task while others are still struggling, encourage the successful teams to jump beyond existing designs and try something really different. Since they have already experienced success, their new forays into more creative solutions won't damage their self-confidence. Suggest that they see how large or small their solution could become or that they try to come up with a new approach that no one else has thought of.

Resist the temptation to give explicit directions. Some students will find the transition from following directions to thinking for themselves to be difficult. You can help them by asking questions that lead them to new insights. Letting students address problems with their ideas, even if you can see that they won't work, is essential to the inventing (and learning) process.

While students are working on mock-ups and encountering problems you can help them to understand the underlying science. Ask questions and demand thoughtful responses before allowing them to continue building. Drawing analogies to experiences they have had will help them form mental connections. Prepare yourself by reviewing the Science Concepts section and Teachable Moments notes of each activity beforehand.

## Raising the Stakes

After students have accepted the challenge and attained some degree of success, the next step is to raise the stakes. Many students will announce that they've made their toy and it works, so they're done. From a learning perspective they've just started when they've made their first model. Your objective is to get them to refocus on the challenge and make improvements to their toy.

Students are used to doing a project once and moving on to the next assignment. However, inventing takes the opposite approach. Inventors know that the first time they craft a solution it won't be the final one; it may not even be close. The most learning occurs when students test their ideas,

find them to be inadequate, and figure out what to do to make their inventions better.

Using a yardstick or meter stick to measure progress towards a defined goal is an excellent way to encourage improvement. A team's car run of 10 feet may be okay until someone else's car goes 15 feet. Measuring results gives both data to analyze and inspiration to other teams. Post the results where everyone can take a look at them. (Although the intent is not to turn the inventing process into a competition, it will fire up the competitive spirit and result in students expending more effort.)

Students will sometimes need constructive criticism in order to improve their designs. One method of providing this is as follows. First, initiate a dialogue by pointing out the positive aspects of the model or the team's work ethic. (For some projects you may need to use considerable imagination, but make sure you start with a positive.) Then ask about the most obvious limitation of the work, being careful to keep the remarks impersonal. When team members agree that their work has one or more limitations, you can then proceed to raise ideas to overcome the limitation. Ask if they have any themselves. Most teams will have a few, which allows you to help them select one or more to pursue. If they don't have any ideas, you may ask if they would like to hear some of yours, but they should have the option of declining. The onus will be back on them to figure out a solution; check back with them a little later to see if they are making progress. This process of providing critical feedback, then, has three phases: positive comments, raising questions about limitations, and raising ideas to overcome the limitations. Although time-consuming, it is an approach that builds, rather than destroys, self-confidence.

### Showcase Success

When a design does exceptionally well, announce it to the class and have the team describe and demonstrate the distinguishing features. Congratulate the team, but focus on the design and why it works. (This is a good time to present a little science content.) Encourage other teams to learn from the demonstrated successes. They shouldn't copy another team's design, but should instead try to understand it and use the information to improve their own designs.

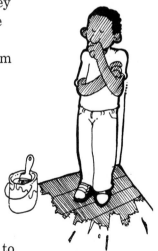

## Connecting the Learning

One reason that toy inventing workshops are such rich learning experiences is that they present many opportunities for students to utilize multiple intelligences. Obviously, individuals who are strong logical-mathematical learners will do well in this type of setting, but students who are stronger in other intelligences—especially the visual-spatial, interpersonal, bodily-kinesthetic, interpersonal, and naturalist intelligences—will also be able to put their own particular abilities to good use. As you plan and conduct a workshop, look for opportunities to accommodate all of the students in your class. For example, you may wish to take multiple intelligences into consideration when you pair students up in teams, or when you choose follow-up activities. (For more on multiple intelligences, see Howard Gardner's description in his 1983 book, *Frames of Mind*, as well as the extensive body of later material on the subject.)

Students will intuitively learn physics as well as science methodology through designing, building, and testing their toys. To maximize the value of the learning, you need to help them recognize what is happening and make sure they acquire appropriate language so that they can express what they have learned. This will enable them to assimilate their understanding and recall the learning to apply it later.

For example, many students have difficulty simply reporting what happened in an experiment. Instead of "the car turned to the right," they may observe that "I messed up," or that "my car is no good." Your first challenge is to get them to watch what happens and to report it accurately. As simple as this is, it is an essential lesson of science.

Students will express their native ideas (including misconceptions) when they design a toy and when they have to explain what happened in an experiment. It is more productive to have them test their ideas than it is to tell them they are wrong. Only when they observe that their understanding is not correct will they be ready to change. When an experiment goes contrary to a student's expectations, help the student to understand what happened by asking questions.

Require students to tell you what happened before they retrieve their vehicle or start a new experiment. If they tell you they didn't see what happened, have them repeat the same experiment again with the understanding that they will report on it afterwards.

A higher-level challenge is to have students associate effects with causes. Once they can describe what is happening, have them tell you why. You want them to start a habit of looking for a cause and making a hypothesis about it. During the first inventing activity you may want to demonstrate the "see an effect, look for the cause" behavior you want them to mimic. With subsequent activities they should search for a cause with little or no prompting from you.

## Culminating the Experience

Culminating projects are a way to "bring it all together" after an inventing workshop. In building and testing their inventions, students develop an intuitive understanding of the pertinent science. They reinforce their understanding when they share their ideas with you and their classmates during a workshop, and when they draw and label their inventions and record their observations and data in their Toy Inventor's Logs. A good final project allows them to package everything they have created and learned and show it off to the world (or at least to their own small corner of it).

You can structure projects to be as multidisciplinary as you want, encompassing history, art, music, or language arts. Workshop-specific suggestions for follow-up and extension are provided in the teaching notes for each workshop. Four "generic" activities are as follows.

### Celebrate Your Own Success

Buy yourself a latte (or whatever reward you give yourself) when students find a possible cause for an effect, form a hypothesis, and design and run an experiment to verify it. Learning to do that will empower them to learn from their own experiences throughout their entire lives. Congratulations!

➤ **Web Pages**

The simplest use of a web page might be as an alternative format for a written report on a student's workshop experience or an assigned topic, but the possibilities for use of this medium of expression are nearly endless. Students love creating their own web pages and will enjoy learning how to do so if they don't already know. Web page creation software makes the job quite manageable, although there are many benefits to having students do it "from scratch," creating an HTML document themselves. (Discussion of the details is beyond the scope of this book, but abundant resources are available in printed books and over the Internet, or there may be students in your class who know how and would be delighted to share their knowledge with their classmates.)

➤ **Science Fairs and Contests**

Students entering their toy inventions in a science fair or contest will have the experience of drawing together everything they learned and communicating it via several different methods. Many of the activities in this book are suitable for science fair projects or could provide good starting points. Some science fairs include a separate

category for inventions. Advise students to read the entry instructions carefully to make sure that their project fits. In addition to science fairs, there are various local, regional, and national contests for inventions. (For a detailed source of information on invention contests, see *How to Enter and Win an Invention Contest,* referenced in the book list in Part III.)

➤ **Oral Presentations**

Team oral presentations are a good way for students to share information and ideas with others. Specify a format, a time limit, and suggested content, such as special features of their toy, test results including a graph of testing data, problems they experienced during the inventing process, design changes they would like to try and why they think they will work, and three (or more) things they learned. After a presentation you can ask the audience if they have questions for the presenters, and you can address questions to them as well.

➤ **Written Reports or Journals**

Using their Toy Inventor's Logs as a starting point, students can prepare written reports that describe their inventions and what they learned in the process of creating them. Provide specific instructions, or let students decide for themselves what they want to put into their reports. Written reports are an ideal vehicle for subject integration.

## Encourage Creative Commercialism

An alternative presentation idea is to have each team create a 30-second television or radio commercial for their toy. They should have to stay within the realm of reality (they can't promise results that the toy can't deliver), but should point out the positive features and the benefits for the buyer.

## Gauging Success (Assessment)

Abundant opportunities for spontaneous, informal assessment will arise during the course of a toy inventing workshop. Simply asking questions while students are engaged in inventing activities and at the conclusion of each activity will give you a fairly good idea of how much they are learning about the science involved. Refer to the Science Concepts section for each activity to help decide what questions to formulate, and judge how confidently and correctly the students respond. Looking at their Inventor's Logs is another way to gauge their learning progress. Tell them before starting a project that you will be checking their logs and will expect to see their creative ideas, illustrations of inventions, diagrams, and key words. In addition, any of the culminating activities described above or the follow-up activities described in workshop notes may be evaluated as a way of assessing student learning.

### Send Them Home for More

Even students who shun homework may willingly work on their inventions at home. The longer they do so the more they will learn, the more skills they will develop, and the more confidence they will acquire. Encourage them to bring in new and improved inventions to demonstrate to the class.

For a more formal evaluation instrument, you may wish to copy and distribute the Toy Inventing Report that follows, or design a written measure that meets your own specific assessment needs.

# Toy Inventing Report

Your team is responsible for preparing and presenting a report on the toy you invented. This is to be a team effort. Your report may be in the form of a web page, a written report with illustrations, or an oral presentation.

Your report must include the following information:

1. **Team name**

2. **Names of team members**

3. **What you invented**

    Give a name to your toy.
    Provide a description in words and photos or illustrations.
    Point out the design features that make the toy work well.
    What ideas do you have to improve the model?

4. **How it works**

    What type of energy does your invention need to operate? (chemical, mechanical, energy of position, heat, sound, light, or other)
    What forces are involved in making your invention work?
    How does the mechanism of your invention work?

5. **How you tested your toy**

    Provide the data from your test.
    Show a graph of the data, making sure you label the graph and include units.
    Write a brief explanation of what the graph shows.

6. **Production**

    What materials did you use to make your toy?
    Would you use different materials if you were going to sell the toy? Why?

7. **The flow of energy from the sun, through your toy, to heat**

    Make a diagram.
    Is your toy energy efficient?

8. **The largest problem your team had to overcome**

    How did you come up with ideas for solutions?

9. **Why someone would want to buy this toy**

10. **The names of each team member and the percentage of work each contributed to this report. Have all team members agree and sign.**

    Team member _____ contributed _____ %

    Team member _____ contributed _____ %

    Team member _____ contributed _____ %

Inventing Toys ©2002 Zephyr Press, Tucson, Arizona • 800-232-2187 • www.zephyrpress.com

# Toy Inventor's Log

**Project name** _____

**Team members** _____

| | |
|---|---|
| **Sketch**<br><br>Sketch your toy design in the space to the right. Label the main parts. | |
| **Materials**<br><br>List materials you will need to make the toy. | |
| **Energy**<br><br>For moving toys, list the energy source. | |

# Toy Inventor's Log *(continued)*

| | |
|---|---|
| **Testing Data**<br><br>What happened in the test and how will you improve the design?<br><br>Make a table and record data from tests. | |
| **Improvements**<br><br>List ideas for improving your toy. | |
| **Knowledge Gained**<br><br>List what you learned that will help you with inventing your next toy. | |

Signed: _____ Date: _____

Witness: _____

Inventing Toys ©2002 Zephyr Press, Tucson, Arizona • 800-232-2187 • www.zephyrpress.com

# Part II
# Workshops

*Any activity that causes students to think and make is good. If the activity causes them to rethink and redo, it's even better . . . When students design, build, use and test their own projects, it's the best that science education gets.*

—Paul Burton, 7th–8th grade teacher
(in *Design as a Catalyst for Learning*)

# Reverse
# ENGINEERING

## Challenge

To experiment in order to test conjectures about internal mechanisms of toys, and then to confirm the findings by taking the toys apart

**WORKSHOP**

# Science Concepts

➤ *Energy Storage*

➤ *Energy Conversion*

➤ *Friction*

➤ *Gears*

➤ *Experimental Design*

➤ *Data Collection and Analysis*

Inventors take things apart to find out how they work. In this activity, students work in teams of two to operate a toy car, think about how it works, and then take it apart to see if their ideas are correct. Reverse engineering gives them good experience in experimental design, thus setting the stage for other workshops in which they will build their own toys and test them.

This activity is a logical setting for introducing concepts and vocabulary related to forces and energy. The toy car that students will be investigating uses a simple spring-based mechanism to operate. The toy user inputs energy into the toy. The energy is stored in the spring, which is released to make the toy work. The car also uses a set of gears, which provides an additional avenue for exploration.

Although sound is not the main topic students will be exploring, the toys do make noise. You could challenge students to think how the sound is generated and dissipated during this activity.

# Standards

| American Association for the Advancement of Science Benchmarks | |
|---|---|
| **Chapter** | **Section** |
| The Nature of Science | The Scientific World View<br>Scientific Inquiry<br>The Scientific Enterprise |
| The Nature of Mathematics | Mathematics, Science, and Technology |
| The Nature of Technology | Technology and Science<br>Design and Systems<br>Issues in Technology |
| The Physical Setting | Energy Transformations<br>Motion |
| The Designed World | Energy Sources and Use |
| Common Themes | Systems<br>Models |
| Habits of the Mind | Values and Attitudes<br>Computation and Estimation<br>Manipulation and Observation<br>Communication Skills<br>Critical-Response Skills |

| National Research Council Science Education Standards | |
|---|---|
| **Content Area** | **Abilities/Understanding** |
| Science as Inquiry—Standard A | Abilities necessary to do scientific inquiry**<br>Understanding about scientific inquiry** |
| Physical Science—Standard B | Properties of objects and materials**<br>Position and motion of objects<br>Motions and forces*<br>Transfer of energy* |
| Science and Technology—Standard E | Abilities of technological design**<br>Understanding about science and technology** |
| Science in Personal and Social Perspectives—Standard F | Science and technology in local challenges<br>Science and technology in society* |
| History and Nature of Science | Science as a human endeavor**<br>Nature of science* |

** denotes standards apply for both K–4 and grades 5–8
* denotes standards for grades 5–8
No mark refers to standards for K–4.

# A Brief History of Springs

By definition, a spring is a piece of material that returns to its prior shape or position after having been bent out of shape. Metals and plastics are typically used in making springs, as both exhibit elastic properties. (*The Way Things Work* has illustrations of several types of springs.)

Many ancient devices, including bows and other devices for launching projectiles, used elastic properties of material. The Egyptians were the first to use metal springs. In 236 BC, Egyptian engineers employed springs to supply the restorative force in catapults.

In the 1500s leaf springs were invented to absorb the shock of the road for people traveling in wheeled carts. In 1675 a Dutch inventor (C. Huygens) invented a clock powered by a spring. Coil springs were invented in the eighteenth century. (To see coil and leaf springs, crawl underneath your car.)

The nineteenth century saw an explosion of innovative use of springs in machines ranging from typewriters to record players. The invention of plastics introduced a cheaper material with elastic properties, allowing even more products to use springs. Although we don't often think about springs, we use them every day to restore switches we push, move the stapler arm back up, adjust seats, close doors, support the open hoods of cars, and hold papers together (paper clips).

Perhaps the most notable spring—although not the most utilitarian one—is familiar to kids across the country. During World War II, Richard James watched an errant spring bounce along the deck of a ship. It gave him the idea for a new toy. His wife, Betty, searched the dictionary for a name and came up with Slinky. That creation launched the James family into the toy business, and they started what is now one of the most successful privately owned toy companies in America.

# Materials

The workshop notes in this section of the book are intended for use with a model of toy car called a pullback car. You can also conduct a Reverse Engineering workshop using the Push 'n Go™ car, a somewhat different model of toy car. (The Push 'n Go car is more expensive but can be reassembled and used again.) If you wish to use Push 'n Go cars, refer to Part III of this book for an adapted version of the workshop notes.

✔ *Pullback cars*

✔ *Small Phillips screwdrivers*

✔ *Small flathead screwdrivers*

✔ *Safety goggles*

✔ *Measuring rules or tapes*

✔ *Masking tape*

✔ *Graph paper*

## NOTES

You can find pullback cars at small toy stores for around $1.00 apiece. You will need to provide one toy car per team of students. It is also desirable if you can provide one Phillips screwdriver for each team. Make sure that the ones you provide fit the small screw on the underside of this toy. The flathead screwdrivers are for use if you choose to have students open up the gear cases on a car.

The goggles are a safety measure. Although the springs in these toys are unlikely to fly out, students should protect their eyes when they are disassembling the cars.

# Using Volunteers

Volunteers can help teams collect data and use tools. If they are not experienced with this type of learning process, you will want to orient them before the activity. In particular, remind them not to take over from the students in an attempt to help teams "get it right." Getting it wrong is often the best way to learn (as long as no damage or injuries occur) and students need to have the opportunity to try their ideas and assess whether their understandings were accurate or not.

# Issuing the Challenge

Use the following script or your own words.

"You may be surprised to hear this, but we've suddenly all changed jobs. This place is no longer a school, it's a toy company! My new job is manager of product development, and I've hired all of you talented inventors as design engineers. The company president [insert name of school principal if desired] has issued a challenge for us today.

"It seems that one of our competitors has a toy car that is selling extremely well, and we may be interested in making and selling a toy like it. We need to understand how their cars work, how we could make something similar, and what we could change to make our version sell better.

"What we want to do today is to try out the cars, predict what makes them go, and then take them apart to confirm our analysis. Later we can try to come up with new designs for the toys."

# Warm-Up

Hold up and then demonstrate a pullback car. Elicit conjectures as to how the toy works, and summarize them on the board. Include ideas whether they are right or wrong. The goal at this point should be just to get students thinking in general terms, not coming up with detailed explanations.

# Procedure

1. **Pair students up in teams and distribute pullback cars.**

   Allow students to play with the toys for a few minutes to get a sense of how the cars operate. Tell them to think about what the inside of the car might look like and what might be happening to make the cars move.

**Teachable Moments**

## ENERGY AND VELOCITY

While students are operating the cars, ask directed questions to stimulate thinking about relevant concepts of physics. For example, ask students if the toys need energy to move. Where does the energy come from? After someone transfers energy to the toy, it is stored internally. How is the energy stored? After it is released, why does the toy eventually stop? Where did the energy go? Does the toy travel at the same speed through a run? Or did it start slowly, build up speed, and slow down? As students answer the questions in their own words, coach them to substitute appropriate vocabulary. For example, "Acceleration is what we call changes in velocity."

2. **Distribute the Experimental Design handout and Toy Inventor's Log.**

   Both handouts are supplied at the end of the notes for this workshop. As directed by the Experimental Design hand-out, students will be conducting an experiment to gather information about how the car works. This should help to prove or disprove their hypotheses about the mechanism. Have them start by recording their ideas about how the car works in their Toy Inventor's Logs.

3. **Have students run the experiment.**

   Students will need measuring devices, masking tape, and graph paper. After collecting and graphing the data, they use the slope of the line to get an estimate for the distance traveled per inch pulled back. The faster the car moves, the more momentum it has (momentum is mass times velocity). At higher speeds the car continues to roll due to its momentum. Thus the graph of the data isn't a straight line; it's curved, and the slope increases as the pullback distance increases.

   If data is collected for longer pullback distances, the graph will change radically. Since the gears disengage at some point of the pullback (to protect the spring), pulling the car farther won't add energy to the spring, so the graph will flatten out at pullback distances beyond the maximum allowed. (Pulling it back 5 feet instead of 5 inches won't increase the distance it travels forward.)

4. **Distribute Phillips screwdrivers and safety goggles and have teams disassemble the cars, then study the internal mechanism.**

   Afterwards, have students use their Inventor's Logs to record what they have learned.

*Teachable Moments*

## CONJECTURING

Generating a hypothesis about a hidden internal mechanism is difficult, and students may need some help. Ask the class to describe how the toy operates. Does the distance the car travels depend on how far they pull the toy back? Does the distance the car travels *equal* the distance they pull it back? Students should be able to recognize that since they pull the car back only a few inches to get it to move forward several feet, there must be a mechanism in the car that multiplies the distance it can travel.

## NOTE

If you choose to have students open the gear boxes of their cars, they will also need flathead screwdrivers. Alternatively, you could study the gear box of one car as a whole-class activity.

### Teachable Moments

### GEARS AND MOTION

After students have observed the gear mechanism, reinforce their learning by asking directed questions. For example, "What do the gears do? What happens when a big gear pushes a little gear? Do the gears speed up or slow down the motion of the drive mechanism?"

# Wrap-Up

Have each team display their graphs, report on their experiences, and tell what they learned. Review the procedures for conducting an experiment and allow students to share how they implemented them.

# Follow-Up Activities

1. Ask students whether each team got the same or similar distance measurements for their pullback cars. Have teams share data and average the data from three different teams for each distance of pullback. Graph the averaged data and see how the graphs compare to students' original graphs.

2. Have students test the cars on different surfaces to learn about friction. For example, if they used the cars on a wooden or concrete floor earlier, have them try with carpet. On what surface does the car travel farthest? Why?

3. Ask students to describe machines in which the direction of motion changes between the driving force (or motor) and the wheels. They may know, for example, that in most cars the up-and-down motion of the pistons is transformed to a rotational motion that is perpendicular to the motion of the wheels.

4. Have students generate a list of toys that use stored energy and tell how the energy is stored. Discuss the different types of storage mechanisms, such as batteries (chemical), rubber bands or springs (mechanical), and elevation (gravitational).

5. Have students work at home to come up with design ideas for a new product, based on their experiences in the workshop.

6. Hand out the Energy Storage Word Search Puzzle (provided at the end of this workshop) and challenge students to find all 21 things that store energy. See Appendix for answers.

# Extensions to Other Subjects

1. Assign students to write the script for a one-minute television commercial promoting pullback cars. Then have them read or act out the commercial for the class.

2. For an art project, have students create covers for their Toy Inventor's Logs. They could illustrate them with drawings of a pullback car (or its inner parts) or with other art related to science concepts or inventing.

# Resources

***The Way Things Work*** (David Macaulay). Shows how many devices work and gives illustrations of several types of springs.

***Young Inventors at Work! Learning Science by Doing Science*** (Ed Sobey). Lists several other activities for reverse engineering.

***Teaching Physics with Toys*** (Beverley Taylor et al.). Suggests several other experiments to run using toy cars.

# Reverse Engineering—Pullback Cars

## Experimental Design

How do you think this toy works? Make a *hypothesis* that includes a statement about what happens when you pull back the car and then release it. Then gather data by conducting an experiment to see how far the car travels when pulled back different distances. Finally, take the car apart to see if you were right.

1. Write your hypothesis about how the car works in your Toy Inventor's Log.

2. Pick a spot on a smooth floor where the car will be able to roll at least 12 feet. Place a short piece of masking tape on the floor to mark your starting position. Place a longer piece of masking tape (about 5 inches long) at right angles to the first one, so it extends away from the area the car will be traveling. On the longer piece of tape make a mark every half-inch, starting from where the tape intersects with the front edge of the shorter piece of tape.

3. Place the car so its rear wheels are on the front edge of the short masking tape. Pull it back until the rear wheels are lined up with the first half-inch mark on the tape. Release the car.

4. When the car has stopped, measure the distance from its rear wheels to the front edge of the short piece of tape. Record your data in your Toy Inventor's Log.

5. Repeat the test at each half-inch mark up to the point where you hear the clicking sound. Remember to record the data.

6. Graph your data. Think about the experiment and the graph. What do you expect to find inside the car now? Did your hypothesis change?

7. Take the car apart. Record what you find in your Inventor's Log. Were you right about how it works?

# Toy Inventor's Log—Reverse Engineering

**Project name** _____

**Team members** _____

| | |
|---|---|
| **Sketch**<br><br>Make a drawing to show how you think the car works.<br><br>Show what turns the wheels. | |
| **Write**<br><br>Record your hypothesis about how the car works. | |
| **Experiment**<br><br>Run an experiment to test your idea about how the car works.<br><br>Record your data. | |

**Sketch**

After you take the car apart, sketch how it works.

Were your ideas close?

**Knowledge Gained**

List what you learned that will help you with inventing a toy.

Signed: _____ Date: _____

Witness: _____

# Energy Storage Word Search Puzzle

| | | | | | | | | | | | | | |
|---|---|---|---|---|---|---|---|---|---|---|---|---|---|
| E | B | L | Y | R | W | X | A | J | R | O | Z | E | D | W |
| R | U | B | B | E | R | B | A | N | D | U | M | G | N | L |
| U | J | C | L | X | B | G | N | I | R | P | S | N | O | S |
| S | D | P | E | A | N | U | T | S | Y | K | D | A | I | T |
| S | D | O | J | D | Y | N | A | M | I | T | E | R | S | E |
| E | X | Q | U | J | D | P | O | S | I | T | I | O | N | A |
| R | E | S | E | R | V | O | I | R | S | K | K | I | E | M |
| P | U | L | E | E | H | W | Y | L | F | P | L | H | T | P |
| R | R | R | H | L | H | D | R | U | E | O | A | F | A | T |
| I | G | B | A | T | T | E | R | Y | S | T | O | M | E | B |
| A | Z | M | D | N | H | R | Q | A | C | A | C | W | H | A |
| X | F | H | S | T | I | R | G | O | K | T | O | V | M | J |
| Y | W | J | J | R | S | U | Q | V | D | O | S | I | V | N |
| P | R | O | G | D | K | L | M | K | D | E | L | A | L | D |

| | | |
|---|---|---|
| air pressure | gunpowder | reservoir |
| battery | heat | rubber band |
| coal | oil | spring |
| dynamite | orange | steam |
| fat | peanuts | tension |
| flywheel | position | uranium |
| gasoline | potato | wood |

# Toy CARS

## Challenge

To create model cars that travel the farthest distance when propelled by gravity down an inclined ramp

WORKSHOP

# Science Concepts

➤ *Measurement and Data Collection*

➤ *Graphing*

➤ *Energy Transformations: Potential to Kinetic to Heat*

➤ *Friction*

➤ *Forces: Gravity*

The making and testing of cars provides natural opportunities for students to conduct scientific investigations. In order to learn how to make their cars go farther, they will get involved in experiment design, data collection, graphing, and interpretation. As they test their models, they will learn about the various factors that impact acceleration and distance traveled. This workshop is a logical setting for learning about gravity, friction, and energy transformations. You can facilitate by introducing appropriate vocabulary and asking questions that stimulate students to think about the relevant concepts of physics: Where did the car get the energy to move to the top of the ramp? Where did *that* energy come from? What kind of energy does it possess before you release it? Does a car have more potential energy when it is at the top of the ramp or in the middle? Where is the kinetic energy the greatest? Why does the car slow down after it leaves the ramp?

# Standards

| American Association for the Advancement of Science Benchmarks ||
|---|---|
| **Chapter** | **Section** |
| The Nature of Science | The Scientific World View<br>Scientific Inquiry<br>The Scientific Enterprise |
| The Nature of Mathematics | Mathematics, Science, and Technology |
| The Nature of Technology | Technology and Science<br>Design and Systems<br>Issues in Technology |
| The Physical Setting | Energy Transformations<br>Motion<br>Forces of Nature |
| The Designed World | Energy Sources and Use |
| Common Themes | Systems<br>Models |
| Habits of the Mind | Values and Attitudes<br>Computation and Estimation<br>Manipulation and Observation<br>Communication Skills<br>Critical-Response Skills |

| National Research Council Science Education Standards ||
|---|---|
| **Content Area** | **Abilities/Understanding** |
| Science as Inquiry—Standard A | Abilities necessary to do scientific inquiry**<br>Understanding about scientific inquiry** |
| Physical Science—Standard B | Properties of objects and materials**<br>Position and motion of objects<br>Heat<br>Motions and forces*<br>Transfer of energy* |
| Science and Technology—Standard E | Abilities of technological design**<br>Understanding about science and technology** |
| Science in Personal and Social Perspectives—Standard F | Science and technology in local challenges<br>Science and technology in society* |
| History and Nature of Science | Science as a human endeavor**<br>Nature of science* |

** denotes standards apply for both K–4 and grades 5–8
* denotes standards for grades 5–8
No mark refers to standards for K–4.

# A Brief History of Cars

Cars were not invented per se; they evolved from several lines of technology. People had used carts and wagons drawn by horses and other animals for centuries. Wheels were invented by 3200 BC and carts were in use by 2700 BC. As steam engines, electric motors, and internal combustion engines were developed, each in turn was fitted into a wagon or cart to replace the beast in front:

- Nicolas Cagnot of France created a three-wheeled steam-powered car in 1770.

- Working independently, in 1885 Gottlieb Daimler and Karl Benz developed gasoline engines, soon used in cars and trucks.

- The first electric car was made in 1890.

- Charles and Frank Duryea (not Henry Ford) made the first successful gas-powered car in America in 1893.

- Rudolf Diesel built and demonstrated the first diesel engine in 1896.

Cars today represent the culmination of thousands of inventions, ranging from pneumatic tires to turn signals.

Toy cars evolved as advances in technology and materials allowed them to become durable and inexpensive. Ruth Handler, who invented the Barbie doll and helped found Mattel Toys®, wanted to get into the model car market in 1967. At her request, toy designers at Mattel made a gravity-powered model. The car so excited Ruth that she exclaimed, "Wow, those are hot wheels," thus providing a name for Mattel's very successful product.

The creators of Matchbox® cars weren't trying to make big inroads into the toy business. They simply wanted to keep their die-casting machines busy during slack periods. Their original business was making electric parts, but when the toy vehicles started selling well, they stopped making parts and focused on making miniature cars.

# Materials

✔ *Car bodies (see note below)*

✔ *Wooden or plastic wheels*

✔ *Wooden dowels ($^1/_4$" diameter), for axles*

✔ *Straws ("fat" ones), for bearings*

✔ *Masking tape*

✔ *Ramp (see note below)*

✔ *Measuring tape or stick*

✔ *Graph paper*

## NOTES

### Car Bodies

For each team of students provide either one block of wood (a 4–6" length of 2x4, 2x2, or 2x1), or an empty single-serving juice box. (Juice boxes are ideal because some students will think to fill them with water to make their cars heavier.) Students may also find other objects to use, and you can encourage them to do that. Ask them why they think one car body will be better than another. (Thoughtful responses could be that one has a smaller profile for drag, one is heavier, or one has a better place to attach bearings.)

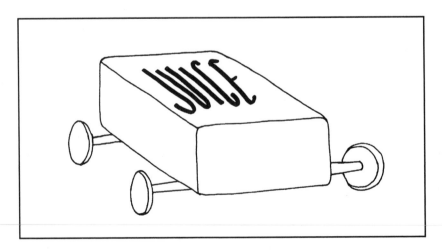

**Students can use a single-serving juice box to make a car.**

## Wheels

Budget four per team. Hobby stores sell bags of wooden wheels for a few dollars. The advantages of these are that the hole for the axle is exactly in the center of the wheel and the wheel is perfectly round. (You may also purchase wheels in bulk, through Woodworks, (800) 722-0311.) An alternative is to have students make wheels out of milk jug lids (or other recycled lids). If you are so inclined, you can also make wheels yourself from plywood, using a hole saw attached to an electric drill.

Ingenious students may venture to try different numbers or positions of wheels. Encourage their experimentation and ask them why their design worked so well (or didn't—creative disasters often have greater learning potential than less-creative successes).

## Axles

Have on hand one dowel (4 feet long) per three or four teams. Quarter-inch dowels cut into appropriate lengths will fit through "fat" plastic straws to serve as axles. (You can purchase the straws at restaurant supply stores.) Students can glue the dowels onto milk jug lids for wheels or jam them into the center hole of wooden wheels (friction or a small piece of masking tape will hold them in place).

## Ramp

Cardboard works well, although it is slippery. If you are planning to do this activity several times, it will be worth the effort to make a wooden ramp.

For a cardboard ramp, open several large cardboard boxes and lay them flat to form a surface at least five feet long and two feet wide. Trim off the excess cardboard, and use duct tape or other strong tape to fasten the boxes together. Arrange the seams so cars rolling down the ramp won't hit a raised edge of the next piece of cardboard.

For a wooden ramp, cut a piece of pine board or plywood 5 to 6 feet long and 12 to 18 inches wide. Tack molding or other wood strips onto the sides of the ramp to keep cars from falling off the sides. Shave (or cut at an angle) the ramp's lower edge so it meets the floor with a minimum gap.

A set of stairs can support the ramp, provided that there is no other foot traffic. You can also prop one end of the ramp on a table and tape it in place. You will need a smooth floor space at least 20 feet long for the run-out.

# Using Volunteers

Volunteers can help throughout the workshop by helping students to measure the distances cars travel and recording the information in a data matrix on the board. If they are knowledgeable in engineering and physical science, they can work with teams suggesting design improvements and asking teams about the science content.

# Issuing the Challenge

Use the following script or your own words.

"Our company Board of Directors has challenged us today to make a new model car. Matchbox and Hot Wheels have dominated the car toy market for years. Now we want to jump in and make some money in this market. We need a hot new idea.

"Right now, we need each team to brainstorm ideas for a model car that children at least five years old could play with. We're targeting a retail price point of under $10, so we're talking about simple models—no remote control. We'll have each team build a model and test it to see how far it travels after being launched from the top of a ramp. Kids will want a car that looks cool and goes far. Today we need to concentrate on making it go far."

# Warm-Up

The day before the workshop, ask students to look for toys at home that use wheels. Have them make a list of these toys. Also ask them to search for patent numbers on the toys and record any they find.

In class, make a list of all the toys they found that use wheels. If any students found patent numbers have them read the numbers to you so you can write them on the board. They can be used to launch a brief discussion of patents and patent applications. (Students may be surprised at how large the numbers are. Explain that patent numbers are issued sequentially, so the highest patent number in existence represents the total number of patents issued by the U.S. Patent and Trademark Office. Students may enjoy comparing and ordering the numbers they brought in and speculating about when the toys were invented. The greater the number, the more recent the patent application.)

Ask students to think about what type of toy car would be fun for a young child to play with. Have them sketch designs and write ideas in their Toy Inventor's Log.

# Procedure

1. **Have students form teams of two or three.**

   If students haven't already formed inventing teams, have them do so now. Letting them choose their own teams is recommended, as long as they form teams that will work well together.

2. **Show the materials available for making the model cars.**

   Students can substitute or add other items if appropriate materials are available. Distribute Toy Inventor's Logs for students to use throughout the activity.

3. **Have each team talk about and then sketch a design.**

   The sketch should show the number and placement of wheels, how they will be attached to the body, and what the body will look like. The name of the car and the names of the designers should also be recorded.

4. **Upon your approval of their designs, let teams pick materials and construct their cars.**

   When a team has sketched a design in a Toy Inventor's Log, have them show it to you for approval. (Remember that it need not be a completely viable design, just one that will provide a fruitful foundation for experimentation.)

   Urge the teams to build rapidly, reminding them that time is money in the toy industry and they should not spend time making the models look nice. When making mock-ups for testing, inventors have to make them as quickly as they can, test them, and then rebuild them based on what they have learned.

Stress the importance of recording ideas in their inventor's log. Such a log not only helps inventors remember their creative ideas, but it will also serve as a legal document that they can use to show that they are the rightful inventors of a toy (especially if the log is signed and dated by the inventors and a witness).

5. **Allow students to test their models and record the distances traveled.**

   Write the names of each car and its designers on the board in a matrix so you can record the distances the cars travel on the test track. Sample data matrix:

| Car Name | Designers | Distance Test #1 | Test #2 | Test #3 |
|----------|-----------|------------------|---------|---------|
| Go-Go Mobile | Jim and Luis | 0 | 10'6" | 15' |
| The Buggy | Kim and Ann | 2'3" | 2'4" | 8'6" |

When a team has a model or mock-up ready, let them test it on the ramp. Instruct them to pull the car so its rear wheels touch the top of the ramp, and to release it without pushing. If possible, have an assistant or volunteer help them measure the distance the car travels from the base of the ramp so you can be free to help teams.

6. **Have students make improvements and continue testing their cars.**

   Before allowing a team to retrieve their car after a test run, ask them to recount what happened in the test. If they can't, have them repeat the test.

## Teachable Moments

### CAUSE AND EFFECT

If a car flips over when it reaches the floor and students are unable to explain what causes this to happen, have them place the car at the bottom of the ramp with the front end just touching the floor. Let them think about it for a while, then ask them to suggest several modifications they could make to stop the car from flipping.

If a car slides down the ramp, ask them why it slides. Have them pick it up and rotate the wheels to see if the wheels or axles are rubbing. If the wheels are sliding down the ramp and students don't know why, have them close their eyes and listen. On hearing the sounds they may know what the problem is.

**Teachable Moments**

## ROADBLOCKS TO LEARNING

Students bring to this activity a host of misunderstandings that may cloud their expectations and detour their learning. To begin with, many aren't used to making objective reports of events. Guiding them to make clear observations and to accurately describe what they have witnessed will build a foundation for them to learn from this activity. From there, a major advance is getting them to recognize that there are understandable causes behind the effects they observe. Many students aren't used to this way of thinking—to them, things just "happen."

Most will be unsure about what force and what energy sources are propelling their cars. Until students have thought about these things for a while and expressed their own ideas, it may not help them to tell them about gravity and the potential energy that they gave the car by lifting it. Let them experiment first. Also, whenever possible have them conduct their own investigations to disprove incorrect understandings, and afterwards have them confirm that their original ideas didn't work.

After a team tests their car and records the data, ask them what would make it travel farther. Some things they could consider include:

- a different arrangement of wheels and axles
- adding or subtracting weight
- making the body more aerodynamic

Remind students to log their design ideas and to record the changes they made that caused the car to travel the recorded distance.

After teams have had the opportunity to test and measure their car's performance at least once (hopefully most teams will make at least three runs), review the data matrix and discuss what design elements gave good results. Give lots of positive feedback to teams that worked diligently, those that tried new ideas, and those that had good success (long travel distances). Ask students to recount the problems they encountered and what they did to overcome them. Weave science content into the discussion as appropriate.

7. **Pick one car to test at ten different ramp positions to demonstrate how potential energy (ramp position) effects kinetic energy and distance.**

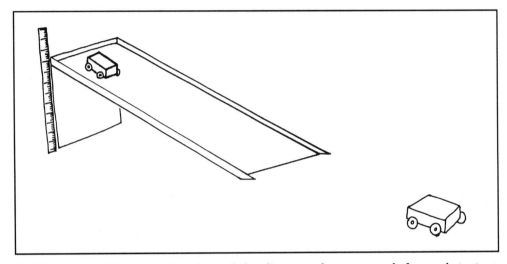

**Students record the ramp height and the distance the car travels for each test.**

Select the car that traveled farthest for additional testing. Ask what features of this car made it travel far. After discussing the features, announce that you want to determine how far it will travel from different launch heights. Assign one student to measure the vertical height of each trial and two students to measure the horizontal distance. The team that created the car can release it for each run. Have the class gather around to witness the demonstration.

## Teachable Moments

### ESTIMATION

After students measure the distance the car traveled, ask them if the measurement looks right. Discuss the value of using estimation to confirm that measurements are reasonable.

After the test runs are recorded, discuss the energy available to propel the car. Why did the car not travel as far when it was started lower on the ramp? What ramp placement gave it the most speed? Ask students to explain how energy is transformed from potential energy (energy of position) to kinetic energy (energy of motion) to heat. Then have students make a graph of the data to show the relationship between the release height and the distance traveled.

# Wrap-Up

Have each team report on their progress and tell what they learned today and what experiments they would try next (at home or on another day at school). Review the procedures for conducting an experiment and allow students to share how they implemented them.

# Follow-Up Activities

1. Try adding a jump to the end of your ramp. Tape a piece of cardboard at the lower edge of the ramp and bend it upward to form a 45-degree angle allowing the cars to "ski jump." Measure the distances achieved and compare them to the launch height on the ramp. Have students predict, then experiment to find the optimal angle for the "ski jump."

2. Challenge students to design various mechanisms to power a car. Use the handout Designing a Propulsion System (supplied at the end of this workshop) to jump-start the creative process.

3. Challenge teams to make model cars that are propelled with a form of energy other than potential energy. For example, they could try balloons, a mousetrap, or an electric motor. Or ask them to design and build model cars driven by a rubber band. (Getting a rubber-band car to travel across a room is a major accomplishment!) Students can compare the distance traveled to the number of turns or twists they give the rubber band, and graph the results.

4. Allow students to create a roller coaster ride for a model car or a ball.

5. Have students complete the Toy Cars Crossword Puzzle (supplied at the end of this workshop). See Appendix for solution.

# Extensions to Other Subjects

1.  Have students design an ad to market their toy car in a children's magazine. Ask them to consider what features would entice kids to buy their model.

2.  Challenge students to guess which car-related toys might be in the National Toy Hall of Fame. Then have them go to the Hall of Fame's web site (www.acgilbert.org) to see if they were right. If they don't see toys they'd expect to find there, challenge them to nominate those toys to the Hall of Fame.

3.  Have students research and report on the people responsible for major innovations to the automobile. A good place to go for information is the web site of the National Inventors Hall of Fame (www.invent.org). Specific inventors to look for include the following:

    | | |
    |---|---|
    | Burton | Kettering |
    | Diesel | Lear |
    | Ford | Otto |
    | Goodyear | Plank |
    | Houdry | Rosinski |

# Resources

***Car Smarts*** (Ed Sobey). Provides creative activities related to cars and car travel, the history of the automobile industry, and the science behind cars, traffic lights, and roads.

***Kid Stuff*** (David Hoffman). Gives the histories of America's favorite toys.

Name _____

# Designing a Propulsion System

Sketch and label at least one design with which you could make a propulsion system for a model car, using the following energy storage systems. Be sure to show how you would get the energy to the wheels that drive the car.

1. A mousetrap

2. A falling weight

3. A battery

# Toy Inventor's Log—Toy Cars

Project name _____

Team members _____

| | |
|---|---|
| **Sketch**<br><br>Sketch your car design in the space to the right.<br><br>How many axles will you use?<br><br>How many wheels will you use?<br><br>Where will you locate the axles? | |
| **Name**<br><br>Come up with a name for your car and write it here. | |
| **Test**<br><br>What happened in the first test?<br><br>How will you improve the design? | |

Inventing Toys ©2002 Zephyr Press, Tucson, Arizona • 800-232-2187 • www.zephyrpress.com

| **Data**<br><br>Record the distances your car traveled. | |
|---|---|
| **Ramp**<br><br>To get your car to go farther, what could you do to the ramp? | |
| **Knowledge Gained**<br><br>List what you learned. | |

Signed: _____ Date: _____

Witness: _____

# Toy Cars Crossword Puzzle

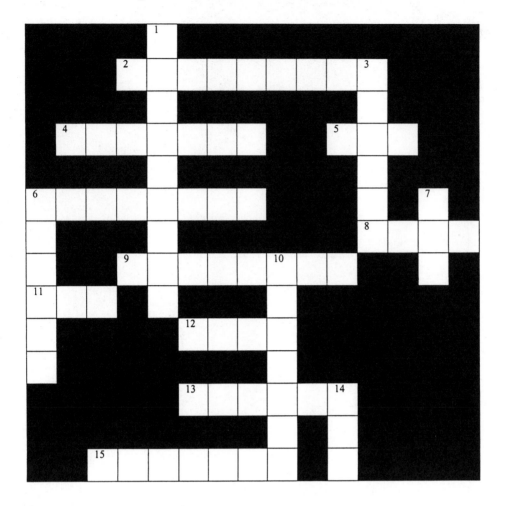

## Across

2. Brand name for cool toy car made by Mattel
4. Energy of motion is called _____.
5. Friction occurs when things _____.
6. Transforms energy of motion into energy of heat
8. Friction causes a car to _____ down.
9. A popular toy car sold in a small box
11. Where to put your car on the ramp to get the longest run
12. When the front axle is turned to the left, in which direction does the car steer?
13. Parts that attach to the axle
15. The force that accelerates a car down the ramp

## Down

1. Energy of position is called _____.
3. Vibrations cause us to hear _____.
6. Starting higher on the ramp causes the car to go _____.
7. After a long car trip, the tires are _____.
10. Energy source for a remote control car
14. The ultimate source of energy for all cars

Inventing Toys ©2002 Zephyr Press, Tucson, Arizona • 800-232-2187 • www.zephyrpress.com

# Toy
## BOATS

## Challenge

To design and build model boats that propel themselves using balloons

**3**

WORKSHOP

# Science Concepts

➤ *Forces and Direction of Forces*

➤ *Energy and Energy Storage*

Making toy boats helps students to understand forces (including buoyancy) and energy. They store energy by inflating balloons, making it natural for you to introduce the concepts of energy storage, energy sources, and energy transformations. Students will exhibit native misconceptions of forces, especially the direction of forces, when they make and test boats. They will learn that to get boats to move in one direction, they must have their balloons vent in the opposite direction.

If time permits, have teams create paddleboats using rubber bands for power. You could also extend the activity to explore the concepts of air pressure, buoyant forces, and electricity (using electric motors for propulsion).

# Standards

| American Association for the Advancement of Science Benchmarks ||
| Chapter | Section |
| --- | --- |
| The Nature of Science | The Scientific World View<br>Scientific Inquiry<br>The Scientific Enterprise |
| The Nature of Technology | Technology and Science<br>Design and Systems<br>Issues in Technology |
| The Physical Setting | Energy Transformations<br>Motion<br>Forces of Nature |
| The Designed World | Energy Sources and Use |
| Common Themes | Systems<br>Models |
| Habits of the Mind | Values and Attitudes<br>Computation and Estimation<br>Manipulation and Observation<br>Communication Skills<br>Critical-Response Skills |

| National Research Council Science Education Standards ||
| Content Area | Abilities/Understanding |
| --- | --- |
| Science as Inquiry—Standard A | Abilities necessary to do scientific inquiry**<br>Understanding about scientific inquiry** |
| Physical Science—Standard B | Properties of objects and materials**<br>Position and motion of objects<br>Motions and forces* |
| Science and Technology—Standard E | Abilities of technological design**<br>Understanding about science and technology** |
| Science in Personal and Social Perspectives—Standard F | Science and technology in local challenges<br>Science and technology in society* |
| History and Nature of Science | Science as a human endeavor**<br>Nature of science* |

** denotes standards apply for both K–4 and grades 5–8
* denotes standards for grades 5 –8
No mark refers to standards for K–4.

# A Brief History of Boats

Boats were one of humankind's earliest inventions, and subsequent history brought a steady stream of improvements by inventors. Archaeologists have identified a paddle, presumably for a boat, that was made around 7500 BC. By 3000 BC, people were using sails to power boats. Around 800 AD, Chinese inventors thought up the rudder. Navigation devices (compasses, sextants, and chronometers) were essential for midocean travel, and their invention spurred exploration and trade. Beginning in 1783 in France and 1787 in the United States, steam power for ships radically changed ocean and river transportation.

In the nineteenth century, John Ericsson made two major contributions to maritime technology: in 1839 he invented the screw propeller that is now used on almost all powerboats and ships, and during the Civil War he designed and supervised the building of the ironclad, USS *Monitor*.

The invention of diesel and gasoline engines at the end of the nineteenth century quickly changed how small boats were propelled. In the early years of the twentieth century, Ole Evinrude applied the new internal combustion technology to rowboats when he invented the outboard engine.

Toy balloons (a boat power source popular with schoolchildren) have an unexpected inventor: chemist Michael Faraday, who is better known for his discoveries in physics and chemistry. He created rubber balloons in 1824 to hold gases that he was generating in his experiments.

Another inventor's name known to most students (at least through association with the eponymous tire company that had no relationship to the inventor) is Charles Goodyear. His discovery of vulcanization in the early 1840s made rubber a much more useful material and made balloons more durable.

Students can find biographies of Ericsson and Goodyear at the National Inventors Hall of Fame website (http://www.invent.org).

# Materials

## Boats

- ✔ *Milk or juice cartons*
- ✔ *Balloons, 10" diameter*
- ✔ *Scissors*
- ✔ *An awl or other sharp tool for poking holes in the cartons*
- ✔ *Dowels, ¼" diameter*
- ✔ *Duct tape*
- ✔ *Straws, bendable*
- ✔ *Rubber bands*
- ✔ *Washers or other small weights (for ballast)*
- ✔ *Paper clips*

## Canal

(to be prepared in advance; see directions at right )

- ✔ *PVC sewer pipe (6" diameter, 12' length), plus 1" pine board, glue, and screws for making end caps*
- ✔ *Alternatively, a plastic rain gutter with end caps*

## NOTES

One milk carton provides boat hulls for two teams. Quart-size cartons work better than half-gallons, as they move through the canal more easily.

The best canal is made of a PVC sewer pipe cut in half lengthwise. To make one, mark where you want the pipe cut by applying lengths of masking tape along the sides, and cut along the tape using a reciprocating saw. Make end caps (dams) for each end by tracing the inside of the pipe onto 1" pine board and cutting it out. Apply a heavy bead of silicon or synthetic glue along the edges of the end caps. Force one cap into each end of the pipe and secure with three or more screws.

Canals made from rain gutters are cheaper and easier to prepare. (You can buy a length of plastic rain gutter and two end caps for just a few dollars.) However, they are narrower, and the smaller width tends to cause boats to get stuck on the sides of the canal, especially if students are using half-gallon cartons.

Either of these canals requires little water to fill (a few bucketfuls) and they are easy to empty. To race boats against one another, build a "portable pond" using pine boards and plastic sheeting. (See *Young Inventors at Work* by Sobey for details.)

# Using Volunteers

Volunteers can set up and fill the canal while students are designing their first boats. They can also help students make the boats by cutting the milk cartons and poking holes for axles, balloons, or straws to protrude through hulls.

As the testing of the boats in the water-filled canal is best done outside and some teams may be working in the classroom while others are testing, volunteers will also be invaluable as activity monitors throughout the workshop.

# Issuing the Challenge

Use the following script or your own words.

"The Toy Factory leadership has decided to get into the toy boat business in time for summer. We want to introduce toy boats that are self-propelled. Since most kids who play with boats will be doing so at swimming pools or ponds, we want boats that are able to navigate at least 12 feet under their own power.

"We have set up a test canal outside so each team can evaluate its design. A successful design will be one that can propel itself at least one length of the canal without a recharge of energy. Of course, we're looking for novel designs of boats and propulsion systems, as long as they can travel the minimum distance.

"To get started, teams will use inflated balloons for propulsion. Successful teams can go on to try propulsion using rubber bands. For test hulls, we have milk cartons, which you may cut in half lengthwise.

"As soon as you have your initial design, come to me for materials so you can start building. When you have built a mock-up, go to the canal outside and test your boat."

# Warm-Up

Have students name all the types of boats and ships they can think of. List all their ideas on the board. Then point out the first item and ask how it is propelled. Write that propulsion system as the first entry in another list, then add all the other boats and ships from the first list that use that propulsion system. For example, under the category "hand-powered boats" you would include canoes, kayaks, rowboats, racing shells, sculls, and poling boats. Other propulsion categories might include steam-powered boats (conventional, paddle wheelers, and nuclear-fueled), diesel- and gasoline-powered boats, sailboats, jet boats, hovercraft, and hydrofoils. Talk about where each type of propulsion is used and why.

To generate ideas about forces associated with balloon-powered boats, have students try to fly balloons across the room by inflating them and releasing the air. See if they can figure out how to get them to travel in a straight line. One solution is to vent the balloon's air through a bendable straw with enough weight attached that the straw drags across the floor, keeping the balloon moving in the same direction. The straw both vents the air and steers the balloon (by frictional drag).

# Procedure

1. **Pair students up in teams and distribute Toy Inventor's Logs.**

2. **Direct each team to make a boat hull.**

   Students can make flat-bottomed boats by cutting a milk carton in half along the sides, or they can make a V-hulled boat by cutting along two opposite edges. (V-hulled boats will require ballast or weight to keep them upright.)

3. **Give each team a balloon and have them design and build a self-propelled boat.**

   A surprising array of design possibilities employ balloons. Balloons can vent either into the air or into the water. They can vent directly from the balloon or through a straw. Straws can pass through a hole in the bottom of the hull or in the stern.

   The most successful designs will probably be those that have the balloon vent into the water through a straw that is constricted by a paper clip. The paper clip slows the flow of air pushing the boat along, conserving energy to complete the trip. (It also results in a realistic outboard motor sound!)

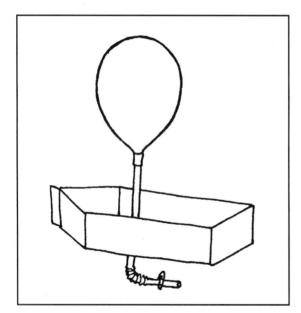

A flat-bottomed boat made from a milk carton

## Teachable Moments

### ENERGY SOURCES

As students are inflating their balloons ask them if the distance their boats travel will depend on the amount of air they store in the balloon. When they are out of breath, ask them what the energy source for their boat is.

4. **Let students test their models.**

5. **If a boat doesn't reach the end of the canal, ask the team to improve it and try again.**

   The most common problem is that the balloon is not venting opposite to the intended direction of travel. Another problem is the boat rubbing on the side or bottom of the canal.

6. **When teams succeed in reaching the end of the canal, let them build a rubber-band powered boat and test it.**

   Once a team has made a boat that travels the length of the canal, have them share their design with others. Then challenge the successful team to change propulsion systems (or add to their existing system) and test again.

   For stern-wheelers, students can make a paddle by notching and fitting together two rectangles cut out of a milk carton. By looping a rubber band over the paddle and onto two supports that extend behind the boat (dowels taped to the sides of the boat), they both support the paddle and provide a way to wind up the rubber band to store energy. Creative students may suggest building a "bow-wheeler" in addition to or in place of a stern-wheeler.

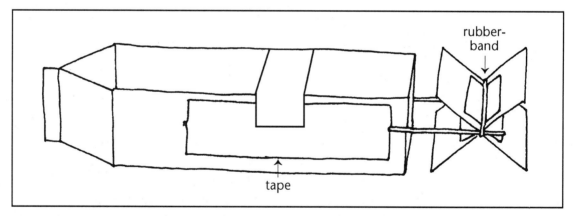

The paddle on a stern wheeler is slipped between the two sides of a rubber band. It can be wound up by rotating it forward around the rubber band. Extending the tape across the open deck of the boat will keep the sides of the boat parallel.

   Side-wheelers require two paddles, one on either side of the boat, attached to a common axle. A rubber band is rolled up on the axle (with the other end attached to the boat). The problem to anticipate is creating a boat too wide for the trough.

   Students could also try several sizes of paddles to see which is most effective, or they could add a second rubber band (or a second balloon).

*Teachable Moments*

## AIR PRESSURE

During the tests, point out how the boats tend to accelerate just before the balloon empties. Ask why that happens. Then ask what stage of blowing up a balloon is the most difficult. The second or third puffs are the toughest because the air pressure inside the balloon is highest then. You can demonstrate this dramatically with the nozzle top from a plastic drinking water bottle. Force a balloon onto the large end of the nozzle and inflate it fully by blowing through the valve. Push the valve shut to capture the air in the balloon. Then blow two or three puffs into a second balloon, and without letting air escape attach it to the other side of the valve. Ask students to predict what will happen when you open the valve. Contrary to common sense, the partially filled balloon will empty into the much larger balloon, because air pressure in a balloon is highest when it is barely inflated.

*Teachable Moments*

## DIRECTION OF FORCES

Students will exhibit native misconceptions about forces, especially the direction of forces, when they make and test boats. Some may have an inflated balloon, attached to the boat, blowing on a sail (also attached to the boat) with the expectation that they will be able to blow their boat along the canal. Others will vent their balloons in the direction of travel (rather than opposite to the direction of travel). When their boats fail to propel themselves, ask them to think about ice skating or roller skating. Have them pretend they are about to start skating. If they want to move forward, what direction do they have to push with their feet? They must push backward to move forward. Have them think about this and then ask them what direction the straw should be facing.

# Wrap-Up

Bring all designing, building, and testing activities to an end and have each team report on their work. Review the native misconceptions and what happened when those ideas were tested. Review the concepts of force and direction of force.

Congratulate teams on their creative attempts and successes. Suggest that some may want to continue experimenting at home and ask them to bring in their next models.

Conclude by having students record in their Toy Inventor's Logs what they learned and what experiments they would try next (at home or on another day at school).

# Follow-Up Activities

1. Challenge teams to propel their boats with a different form of energy. Can they design a boat that runs on water falling out of a cup? How about using an electric motor to propel the boat? Can they design and build a model?

2. Hand out the Ships Word Search Puzzle (provided at the end of this workshop) and challenge students to find all 40 nautical terms. See Appendix for answers.

# Extensions to Other Subjects

Have students create a web page for their boat. They could include links to nautical sites or ocean research centers.

# Resources

***Young Inventors at Work! Learning Science by Doing Science*** (Ed Sobey). Contains stories about some of the inventors whose work involved ships and boats. The book also illustrates one design for a rubber-band-powered boat, and shows how to construct a test tank for racing boats.

***Wacky Water Fun with Science*** (Ed Sobey). Describes several other boat models to build, along with science demonstrations related to water.

# Toy Inventor's Log—Toy Boats

**Project name** _____

**Team members** _____

| | |
|---|---|
| **Sketch**<br><br>Sketch your boat and show how you will have it propel itself. | |
| **Name**<br><br>Come up with a name for your boat and write it here. | |

| | |
|---|---|
| **Energy Storage**<br><br>List other ways to store energy that could propel your boat.<br><br>Sketch designs of how you would make each. | |
| **Testing Data**<br><br>What happened in the test and how will you improve the design? | |
| **Knowledge Gained**<br><br>List what you learned. | |

Signed: _____ Date: _____

Witness: _____

# Ships Word Search Puzzle

| E | R | R | E | C | A | P | T | A | I | N | E | T | A | M |
|---|---|---|---|---|---|---|---|---|---|---|---|---|---|---|
| S | E | E | L | D | D | A | P | A | B | E | A | M | Z | R |
| U | N | M | M | K | L | K | M | B | O | W | L | I | N | E |
| O | I | A | C | M | C | K | A | C | A | B | L | O | E | K |
| H | A | E | C | A | A | R | R | A | T | U | E | E | S | N |
| T | T | T | M | Y | E | J | T | B | S | O | K | F | K | A |
| O | N | S | A | L | P | U | D | I | W | Y | R | G | I | T |
| L | O | K | W | Y | K | E | O | N | A | C | O | I | P | L |
| I | C | A | M | A | I | N | S | A | I | L | N | G | P | I |
| P | R | O | P | E | L | L | E | R | N | W | S | P | E | A |
| T | E | E | G | D | I | R | B | R | E | D | D | U | R | S |
| I | L | D | D | H | A | T | C | H | O | L | D | R | E | D |
| V | A | C | O | N | V | O | Y | A | C | H | T | S | P | N |
| A | H | C | P | Y | E | L | L | A | G | S | T | E | M | A |
| D | W | P | I | L | O | T | E | K | C | A | P | R | R | H |

| | | |
|---|---|---|
| beam | hatch | skipper |
| boatswain | hold | smack |
| bowline | kayak | snorkel |
| bridge | lifeboat | steamer |
| buoy | mainsail | stem |
| cabin | mate | tanker |
| canoe | packet | tender |
| captain | paddle | tramp |
| container | pilot | trawler |
| convoy | pilothouse | whaler |
| davit | propeller | windjammer |
| galley | purser | yacht |
| gig | rudder | |
| hand | sail | |

# Pneumatic-Blast ROCKETS

## Challenge

To build paper rockets that travel as far as possible when propelled by compressed air from a 2-liter bottle

**4**

WORKSHOP

# Science Concepts

➤ *Forces of Flight:*
  *Drag, Lift, and Gravity*

➤ *Energy Transformations*

➤ *Motion: Trajectories*

➤ *Measurement and*
  *Data Collection*

Launching pneumatic-blast rockets gives students a visceral feel for energy transfer. By stomping on a 2-liter bottle they transform the energy in their muscles to the kinetic energy of the rocket. The harder they stomp, the farther the rocket will fly.

Landing on the bottle suddenly compresses the air inside, which blasts out of the launch tube, propelling the rocket. By most definitions this is not a true rocket; it doesn't have fuel or an engine on board that propels it forward. Rather, it relies on the explosive blast of air, much like an artillery shell. (In the case of a shell, the propelling gases are generated in the chemical reaction of explosives in the chamber of the gun.)

By measuring the angle of launch, students can experiment to find the angle that optimizes the range of the rockets (approximately 45 degrees). They can collect data using one or more rockets, graph the data, and then make estimates of the optimal angle.

Students can experiment with adding drag in the form of fins to give their rockets stability. They can also experiment with spin by orientating the fins at an angle to the long axis of the rocket.

# Standards

| American Association for the Advancement of Science Benchmarks | |
|---|---|
| **Chapter** | **Section** |
| The Nature of Science | The Scientific World View<br>Scientific Inquiry<br>The Scientific Enterprise |
| The Nature of Mathematics | Mathematics, Science, and Technology |
| The Nature of Technology | Technology and Science<br>Design and Systems<br>Issues in Technology |
| The Physical Setting | Energy Transformations<br>Motion<br>Forces of Nature |
| The Designed World | Energy Sources and Use |
| Common Themes | Systems<br>Models |
| Habits of the Mind | Values and Attitudes<br>Computation and Estimation<br>Manipulation and Observation<br>Communication Skills<br>Critical-Response Skills |

| National Research Council Science Education Standards | |
|---|---|
| **Content Area** | **Abilities/Understanding** |
| Science as Inquiry—Standard A | Abilities necessary to do scientific inquiry**<br>Understanding about scientific inquiry** |
| Physical Science—Standard B | Properties of objects and materials**<br>Position and motion of objects<br>Motions and forces*<br>Transfer of energy* |
| Science and Technology—Standard E | Abilities of technological design**<br>Understanding about science and technology** |
| Science in Personal and Social Perspectives—Standard F | Science and technology in local challenges<br>Science and technology in society* |
| History and Nature of Science | Science as a human endeavor**<br>Nature of science* |

\*\* denotes standards apply for both K–4 and grades 5–8
\* denotes standards for grades 5–8
No mark refers to standards for K–4.

# A Brief History of Pneumatics and Rockets

Pneumatic systems (systems that operate by air or air pressure) are used today in a wide range of applications, from jackhammers, impact wrenches, and dentist drills to those pneumatic tubes that carry your money from your car at the drive-up window at the bank. This last application—the transfer of cylinders containing documents or other objects—was actually how the technology got started.

The first pneumatic system was built in 1822 to carry telegrams to and from the stock exchange in London. With this system, much like the systems used today, the messages were stuffed inside a cylinder that was sucked to its destination. In 1868 a similar system was built in Paris, and it was used there for a century. This was an impressive system, extending for some 250 miles.

The Chinese pioneered explosive rockets, although there is some disagreement as to when they first employed them. In the early years of the sixteenth century a notable attempt was made to use rockets to make a flying machine. Wan Hu, a Chinese scientist, tested his device with the unfortunate result that it exploded, killing him.

Major advances in rocketry waited until the nineteenth century, when British scientist William Hale added three fins to rockets, giving them greater stability in flight. The twentieth century brought forth notable advances from Robert Goddard and Wernher von Braun.

Goddard is recognized as the father of modern rocketry. When he started his work, public skepticism was so strong that he conducted his experiments in private to avoid scorn. He developed the first mathematical theory of rocket propulsion and proved that rockets could work in the vacuum of space.

Von Braun finished his doctorate just in time to work for the German military prior to World War II. He became the technical director of their rocket development efforts that resulted in the V-2 rocket. After the war he came to the United States, where he eventually led the U.S. ballistic missile program.

# Materials

## Launchers

✔ *2-liter soda bottles*

✔ *Bicycle inner tubes*

✔ *Duct tape*

✔ *PVC pipe, 3/4" diameter, cut into 12" lengths (schedule 200 pipe)*

✔ *Protractor, string, and weight*

## Rockets

✔ *Scrap office paper (8 1/2" x 11")*

✔ *Card stock paper, business cards, and other paper*

✔ *Masking tape, 1" wide*

✔ *PVC pipe, same type as for launchers*

✔ *Scissors*

✔ *Paper clips*

## Measuring Devices

✔ *Meter sticks, measuring tapes, or yardsticks*

## NOTES

The compression chamber for the rocket launchers is a 2-liter bottle. Although these are made of tough plastic, they do wear out after 20 to 40 launches, so you will want to make several launchers and keep extra bottles on hand to replace those that wear out. Bottles will last longer if you restrict students to stomping with one foot only.

Ask your favorite bike store for about a dozen used bicycle inner tubes—the ones they are going to discard. They should be willing to provide these to you at no charge. (Make your request at least a week before you will need them as it may take a store several days to collect them.)

To assemble the launcher, cut a length of inner tube at least 2 feet long. Make sure the section of tube you use isn't one with a hole in it. Stretch one end over the mouth of a 2-liter bottle and tape it in place with about 6 inches of masking tape. Wrap the tape tightly. Stretch the other end of the inner tube onto a 12-inch section of PVC pipe. Use duct tape to secure this end. This completes the assembly of your launcher.

## NOTES

If desired, you can substitute water rockets for pneumatic-blast rockets. To do this you will need a water rocket launcher, 2-liter bottles, and a bicycle pump with a pressure gauge on it. (You can purchase a launcher from educational and scientific catalogs or make one with plans found in *Fantastic Flying Fun with Science* by Sobey.) The disadvantages of using water rockets are the added expense, the increased danger of an accident, and the increased difficulty of making good measurements. Among the added benefits are that they enable students to experiment with adding parachutes, incorporating an aerodynamic nose cone, increasing the mass of the rocket (adding modeling clay or a water balloon to the nose cone), measuring the pressure, and comparing the pressure to the distance the rocket flies.

Because pneumatic-blast rockets are much cheaper and easier to use and because you can use them indoors (in a gym or other large open space), they are recommended as the first choice.

# Using Volunteers

You can use volunteers to operate the launchers, to help measure the flight distances of rockets, and to record the data. As students should operate the launchers only with adult supervision, having volunteers will enable you to have at least two launchers going. Volunteers can ensure that the testing range is free of bystanders, and that the rockets are aimed appropriately. They can also reduce measuring times by marking off the test range ahead of time, leaving short pieces of masking tape every five feet downrange and writing the distance on each piece. (The testing range should be at least 100 feet long. It can be set up outdoors or in a large indoor space such as a gymnasium or lunchroom.)

# Issuing the Challenge

Use the following script or your own words.

"The Toy Factory management has decided that the company wants to sell rockets, and it is our job to find the optimal design. We want our rockets to fly as far as possible. When we have found the design that flies the farthest, we will test it to determine the optimal angle for launching. We will collect this data and graph it. Then each team will get one chance to shoot their rocket off at the optimal angle."

# Warm-Up

A day or two before the workshop, give students a homework assignment of making straw rockets at home. The basic model involves simply launching the straw wrapper off a straw by quickly exhaling. A more advanced model (and one not dependent on wrapped straws) is to make a fuselage by rolling a piece of paper (one-third of a sheet of office paper will do nicely) around a pencil and taping it in place. After the rocket is removed from the pencil, a nose cone can be shaped by crimping one end and taping it. Students place the rocket on a straw and launch it with a gust of exhalation. To fly very far the rocket will require the addition of paper fins. For more on making straw rockets, see *Young Inventors at Work* by Sobey. Alternatively, students can make "match rockets." (See *Fantastic Flying Fun with Science* by Sobey for details.)

In class, allow students to discuss their experiences with these homemade rockets, including any ways they discovered to make the rockets fly farther.

**Rocket testing captures everyone's attention.**

# Procedure

1. **Pair students up in teams. Distribute Toy Inventor's Logs and materials and have teams make rocket fuselages.**

   Using a piece of ³/₄" PVC pipe as a form, students roll a piece of paper around the pipe (aligning the paper either as portrait or landscape), loosen the fit enough to remove the pipe, and tape the resulting paper tube securely with masking tape. To form the nose of the rocket, they push in on opposite sides of one end of the rocket with their opposing forefingers. With the two opposite sides almost touching, they pinch both sides of the nose between both thumbs and middle fingers and secure with a piece of tape. Then they fold the top over and tape it in place to ensure a good air seal. To test for leaks, they should blow air into the open end of the rocket.

2. **Allow students to test their initial models.**

   You can launch the first models in a classroom, because they won't go very far. To launch, slide the rocket onto the PVC pipe that is part of the launcher. As you hold the PVC pipe in one hand (at an angle nearly parallel to the ground if you are in a small room), have a student stomp on the 2-liter bottle with one foot. Emphasize to the nonstomping partner that he or she should watch the rocket, not the launcher.

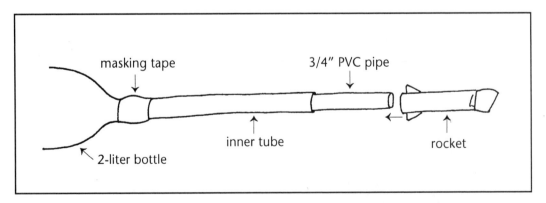

**The rocket slides onto the assembled launcher.**

Rockets without fins will tumble in flight and travel only a few yards. Ask each team after their launch, "What happened?" Get them in the habit of observing, trusting their observations, and being able to verbalize them. Ask them what they need to do to get a longer flight. If they are stuck, ask them to draw a picture of a rocket from memory and to compare their drawing to the rocket they made.

3. **Challenge the students to improve their rockets.**

   Students can add fins in seconds by taking a piece of masking tape and folding it nearly in half so that most of the tape sticks to itself but a sticky edge is left for attaching the fin to the fuselage. Better fins can be crafted from card stock, business cards, or paper. Simple to construct are business-card fins: cut a card in half diagonally and tape each half to the bottom of the rocket.

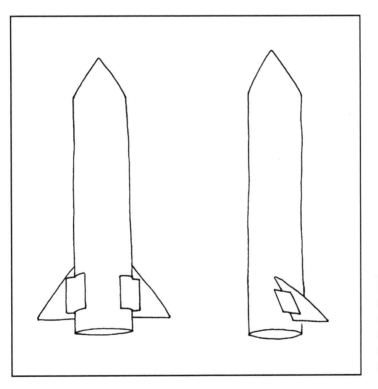

**Fins fixed parallel to the sides of the rocket will cause flight with minimal spin or spiral. Fins set at an angle will cause the rocket to spin in flight.**

Large fins will add enough drag to slow the rocket. The art of making fins is making them large enough to provide stable flight without adding any more drag than is necessary. Fins set at an angle will spin the rocket ("like a quarterback throwing a football"). Fins set at opposing angles add so much drag that the rocket will fall after a short distance.

4. **Allow students to test their enhanced models.**

A large testing range is now needed. Give each team a practice run first, then start measuring distance traveled on the second launch for each rocket. Post the data for all of the test launches on the board or on a flip chart where everyone can see it. Also have students record their own rocket's distances in their Inventor's Logs. In addition, they should record their best designs, sketching the number and placement of the fins and any other attachments. They should also record any ideas they have for making their rockets travel farther.

Have teams share their creative and successful designs with other teams so all can learn what works and what doesn't. Celebrate creative failures as well as successes.

When all the rockets have been tested, gather everyone around to examine the data. Select the two or three rockets that flew farthest and ask what design features were common to them. Discuss other designs and why they did or did not succeed. Keep the talk focused on the designs, not on the individuals who made the designs.

**Teachable Moments**

## ENERGY TRANSFORMATION

After a student has jumped on the bottle, ask where the energy came from to launch the rocket. Use directed questioning as needed to elicit from students the full path the energy took, starting with the sun and ending up with the rocket lying on the ground. They should be able to explain that the sun radiates energy used by plants on earth to convert inorganic compounds into organic compounds we eat as food, that we digest the food energy and store it in our muscles, and that we use some of this energy to jump on the bottle, thereby compressing the air that drives the rocket. Finally, the energy is converted to heat by the rocket sliding through the air.

*Teachable Moments*

## WATCHING A FLIGHT

Have teams describe the flight of their rockets each time. Ask them what forces caused the motion they witnessed. Have teams relate design features to the motion of their rockets. Ask if each trial of a rocket will result in exactly the same distance flown. Ask them what outside factors might influence the flight (for example, wind or variations in stomping).

5. **Ask students to find the optimal angle for launching for distance.**

   Repeat launches of one rocket at a variety of angles from 0 to 90 degrees. You can gauge the angles by using a protractor with string and weight (to orient it vertically) or by taping a protractor to a chair or table for reference and having one student hold the launch tube at the desired angle during each launch. (Alternatively, you can make a variable-angle launch pad consisting of a vertical pine board with a protractor mounted to one side. The PVC launch tube is centered on the protractor so you can read the angle of a launch. A bolt holds the PVC launch tube in place and allows you to hold the angle until you loosen the nut and move the tube. See page 63.)

   Start with small angles (close to 0 degrees or horizontal) and launch the selected rocket. Have two students measure the distance of flight and have another record it on a data form along with the angle. After the data is collected, have students graph it. Ask which angle gives the longest range. (The data will probably support a 45-degree angle.)

   For a fun conclusion, set the launch device for the optimal angle and aim the launcher so each team can try to launch their rocket over the school. Be sure that there are no bystanders in the probable landing area.

# Wrap-Up

Bring all rocket activities to an end and ask students to discuss their experiences and what they learned. Encourage them to continue the activity at home and to report on any great rocket designs they come up with.

# Follow-Up Activities

1.  Challenge students to find out if adding weight (paper clips) would make their rockets fly farther. How would they be able to demonstrate to a skeptic that adding weight gave longer distance? Alternatively, have teams try adding paper or cardboard flaps to their rockets to see what effect drag has.

2.  Find the local rocket club and invite its members to put on a demonstration. Contact local hobby stores to find out who the rocket enthusiasts are. Or ask physics teachers at high schools or local community colleges.

# Extensions to Other Subjects

1.  Have students research Robert Goddard, the father of modern rocketry.

2.  Have students create a rocket report in HTML format. Content could include rocket history, how rockets work, and how rockets help people.

# Resources

***Fantastic Flying Fun with Science*** (Ed Sobey). Describes several other flying toys students can make.

# Toy Inventor's Log—Pneumatic-Blast Rockets

Project name _____

Team members _____

| | |
|---|---|
| **Record**<br><br>Describe the procedures for making rockets and a rocket launcher. | |
| **Materials**<br><br>List materials needed to make a launcher. | |
| **Data**<br><br>Record the distance your rocket flew in each test. | |

| | |
|---|---|
| **Design**<br><br>What arrangement of fins gave the best flights?<br><br>Sketch it. | |
| **Improvements**<br><br>List ideas for improving your rocket. | |
| **Knowledge Gained**<br><br>List what you learned. | |

Signed: _____ Date: _____

Witness: _____

Inventing Toys ©2002 Zephyr Press, Tucson, Arizona • 800-232-2187 • www.zephyrpress.com

# Toy PLANES

## Challenge

To make and fly model airplanes with controllable surfaces

**WORKSHOP**

# Science Concepts

➤ *Forces of Flight: Drag, Lift, and Gravity*

➤ *Direction of Forces*

➤ *Motion: Trajectories*

Having students make, test, and modify planes helps them understand how planes fly. In fact, the best way to understand the forces of flight is to play with a model plane and think about what's happening. The art of flying lies in balancing these forces by making adjustments to the control surfaces so the plane executes smooth turns.

It isn't immediately obvious how changing the control surfaces (rudder and ailerons) impacts flight. With the rudder at the aft of the plane, air hitting predominantly on one side will push the rear of the plane towards the other side. Thus, when the rudder is turned to the left, moving air will push the rudder (and the rear of the plane) towards the right. Pushing to the right at the back of the plane causes the front to turn to the left.

Pushing the wing flaps or ailerons up pushes the back of the wing down and the nose up, causing the plane to climb. Fighting gravity, it soon stalls (has no air moving over the wings to give it lift) and crashes. Pushing the flaps down causes the nose to go down. Pushing one flap up and the other one down results in a roll.

# Standards

| American Association for the Advancement of Science Benchmarks ||
| Chapter | Section |
| --- | --- |
| The Nature of Science | The Scientific World View<br>Scientific Inquiry<br>The Scientific Enterprise |
| The Nature of Technology | Technology and Science<br>Design and Systems<br>Issues in Technology |
| The Physical Setting | Motion<br>Forces of Nature |
| Common Themes | Systems<br>Models |
| Habits of the Mind | Values and Attitudes<br>Computation and Estimation<br>Manipulation and Observation<br>Communication Skills<br>Critical-Response Skills |

| National Research Council Science Education Standards ||
| Content Area | Abilities/Understanding |
| --- | --- |
| Science as Inquiry—Standard A | Abilities necessary to do scientific inquiry**<br>Understanding about scientific inquiry** |
| Physical Science—Standard B | Properties of objects and materials**<br>Position and motion of objects<br>Motions and forces* |
| Science and Technology—Standard E | Abilities of technological design**<br>Understanding about science and technology** |
| Science in Personal and Social Perspectives—Standard F | Science and technology in local challenges<br>Science and technology in society* |
| History and Nature of Science | Science as a human endeavor**<br>Nature of science* |

** denotes standards apply for both K–4 and grades 5–8
* denotes standards for grades 5–8
No mark refers to standards for K–4.

# A Brief History of Planes

The Wright brothers' most significant contribution to the development of the airplane was controlling flight by bending the surfaces of the wings. Being avid bicyclists, the Wrights understood that you can't turn a bicycle merely by rotating the steering wheel. As your students will know, when they want to turn their bikes they have to lean into the turn or they will crash to the outside. Applying this knowledge to the airplane, Wilbur and Orville invented a system to lean or bank the plane when the rudder was turned so the plane could lean into the turn.

If you watch the wings of a modern airliner you will see that the Wright brothers' method, called "wing warping" or bending the wing, is not used today. Actually, the method invented by the Wright brothers was supplanted early on by the modification currently in use, the aileron. Glenn Curtis, an inventor, motorcycle racer, and gasoline engine manufacturer, invented the aileron. He worked with Alexander Graham Bell to create the June Bug, the first plane to fly without wing warping. His innovation, which bypassed the Wright brothers' patent, involved making small flaps on the wing. (The word aileron is French for "small wing.") The Wright brothers believed that this invention was a derivative of their invention, and they sued. However, before the case could be settled in court, World War I forced the two competitors to work together to turn out planes for the military.

# Materials

✔ *Styrene food trays*

✔ *Scissors*

✔ *Rulers*

✔ *Pens*

✔ *Paper clips*

✔ *Masking tape*

✔ *Measuring tape or stick*

### NOTES

You can collect styrene trays, normally used to package meats and sometimes produce items, from a grocery store. Some stores will donate trays or charge you a minimal fee for them. If you have to purchase them, check with restaurant supply stores. Be sure to have plenty on hand, as each team may go through several.

You could use paper instead of styrene, but this is not recommended. Styrene is much better because it holds bends in the wings and tail and is different enough from paper to level the playing field for your inventors. (Experienced paper-airplane flyers will have too great an advantage if you use paper.)

# Using Volunteers

Volunteers can help measure the distances flown and record the data. Have them lay out the test range by marking distances from the launch line. (They could do this by writing measured distances on pieces of masking tape and taping them to the ground.)

As the testing of planes is best done outside or in a large indoor space such as a gymnasium or lunchroom, volunteers will also be invaluable as activity monitors throughout the workshop.

# Issuing the Challenge

Use the following script or your own words.

"The Toy Factory leadership wants us to create a line of toy planes that kids can fly. We will use a lightweight material called styrene for the body of the plane. We need to figure out how to make planes that can fly far, what tricks kids will be able to do with them, and what kind of directions we will supply for using the planes.

"The first goal after building a basic model will be to make adjustments so it can fly farther. The second goal will be to add flaps on the wings and a rudder on the tail so we can control the flight. Finally, we want to write instructions that could go with the toy planes we create. Each member of a team will write instructions for one maneuver and share the written instructions with other team members who will read and critique them. The final instructions for the plane should be complete and easy to understand."

# Warm-Up

Begin by talking through the experience of turning a bicycle so everyone appreciates the importance of leaning into the turn. Then ask how a plane could lean. (In a turn to the left, the plane will need to raise the right wing and lower the left wing. So in effect, the question becomes how do you get an aerodynamic surface—i.e., a wing—to rise or fall.)

The simple answer is you give the wing more lift to rise and more drag to fall. For example, for a turn to the left, you raise the flap (or aileron) on the right wing to gain more lift. Raising the flap causes more air to impact the flap, driving the rear of the model down and the nose up. The flap on the left wing, meanwhile, is lowered to generate more drag. Moving air impacting the underside of the flap will push it upward, driving the nose down.

The coupled motion of the wings, one wing up and the other down, along with a slight leftward bend in the rudder on the tail, will turn the plane to the left. (The idea is simple, but getting all three parts to work at the optimal angles so a smooth turn occurs is difficult.)

# Procedure

1. **Distribute the Toy Inventor's Log for Planes and the handout Flight Characteristics of Toy Planes, then pair students up in teams to make basic models.**

Students will use the log and the handout (both supplied at the end of the notes for this workshop) throughout the activity. As directed by the handout, students will cut the wing and tail of a plane from the flat bottom of a styrene tray, then notch the two pieces so they fit together snugly. Some students will already know exactly how to do this, but other students may need a little assistance. Have teams test-fly their models and report to you how they flew. The emphasis at this stage is on getting a basic operational model in hand.

In most cases the model won't fly at all at first—the nose will rise as soon as the plane is released. When teams report this to you, ask them what they could do to stop the nose of the plane from rising. (Of the several possible solutions, the easiest to try is adding a weight to the nose; with the addition of one or more paper clips, the planes should fly.)

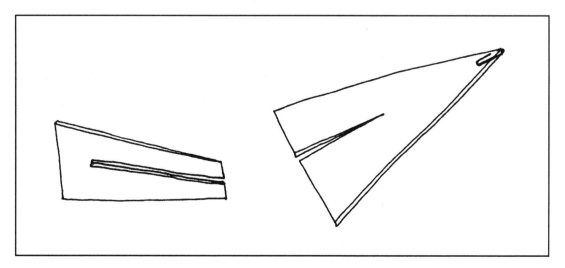

Notch the wing and tail pieces so they will fit together snugly.

2. **Allow teams to test their planes for distance.**

   If possible, measure distances along a straight line from the launch position towards the far end of the test area so students can quickly read and record how far their planes traveled. Prepare a data grid on the board or on a flip chart to record the data as well.

   Students can try adjusting their designs to improve their flight distances. You can also suggest experiments involving more weight or weight added in different places on the plane. Have students record new distance data and any discoveries they report from these experiments.

3. **Have students experiment with aerobatics.**

   When a team has made three measurements of the distance flown, suggest that they modify their plane for aerobatics. They can make one cut in the tail of the model for a rudder, and one cut in each wing for ailerons or flaps. Students adjust the rudder and ailerons by bending the styrene upward or downward slightly. (It is easy to break the styrene by bending, so caution them to adjust the surfaces with small bends.)

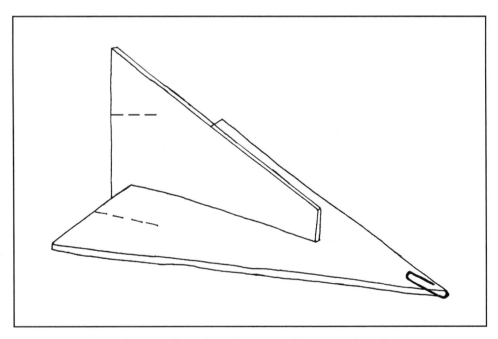

Cutting and gently bending the ailerons will cause the plane to turn.

### Teachable Moments

## CAUSE AND EFFECT

When a plane performs an interesting maneuver, hold the model up for everyone to see and have the designers demonstrate the maneuver. Ask its designers what design elements produced the flight characteristics. This is a good place to weave in appropriate science content.

4. **Challenge students to refine their models to achieve smooth turns.**

   Aerobatic maneuvers are fun, but the real challenge is to adjust the rudder and ailerons so a plane can execute a smooth turn. Ask students to find out what happens if they in turn adjust only the rudder, bend both ailerons upward, bend both ailerons downward, and bend one aileron up and the other one down.

   To turn, they will need to adjust both the rudder and the ailerons. For example, a left turn is achieved by bending the rudder to the left. (Protruding on the left side of the plane, the rudder will force the plane to rotate to the left.) Raising the aileron on the right wing pushes that side upward, and lowering the left aileron causes the left wing to dip. It will take students a few tries to get the exact combination of rudder and aileron adjustments to make a smooth turn, but the process teaches them how a pilot uses control surfaces.

5. **Have students write instructions telling a user how to make the plane turn or climb.**

   Have each student pick one maneuver and write instructions for a buyer of a toy airplane. As a check, each can have another student read the instructions to see if they are understandable.

# Wrap-Up

Conclude by checking the data and asking teams that had great success in distance what made their planes work. Ask if any team succeeded in having their plane execute a smooth turn. Have them demonstrate a turn, explaining what they had to do to achieve it.

Have students record how they made the plane fly up, down, and to the left or right. If they haven't already done so, have them sketch the plane and label the parts, including the control surfaces (rudder and ailerons) in their Toy Inventor's Logs.

# Follow-Up Activities

1. Have teams experiment with large deflection angles on the control surfaces or have them add additional drag surfaces (i.e., a piece of paper taped to the wing so it sticks up from the plane). Discuss the impact of drag on flight.

2. Suggest that students try making control surfaces on their favorite paper airplane models to see if they can get them to turn.

3. Have students look up airplanes in an encyclopedia or in *The Way Things Work* by Macauley to learn more about the parts of the plane and how they work.

# Extensions to Other Subjects

1. Airplanes have had major impacts on how we live and on how we view our world. Have students research and think about these impacts by comparing life before planes were invented to life after. They could consider how planes changed warfare, mail service, acute medical care, or knowledge about our environment.

2. Suggest one of the following aviation pioneers for students to research. They could prepare a web page report or an oral report, with emphasis on how the subject contributed to the progress of flight.

   • Wilbur and Orville Wright
   • Glenn Curtis
   • Charles Lindbergh

- Count Ferdinand von Zeppelin
- Amelia Earhart
- Calbraith Rogers (the first person to fly across the United States)
- Chuck Yeager

## Resources

***Fantastic Flying Fun with Science*** (Ed Sobey). Offers kids a variety of flying toys to build and experiments to try.

***Just Plane Smart*** (Ed Sobey). Written for kids who are riding in airplanes. It gives the history and lore of flying and recommends science activities for young fliers.

***Science from Your Airplane Window*** (Elizabeth A. Wood). Has a wonderful collection of more advanced science activities.

***Super Flyers*** (Neil Francis). Shows how to make styrene planes and numerous other models.

***The Way Things Work*** (David Macaulay). Has good illustrations of how an airplane works.

Name _____

# Flight Characteristics of Toy Planes

What design features make planes fly far? How can we make them do aerobatics? Let's find out using model planes made from styrene.

### 1. Basic Construction

Cut three triangles out of the flat bottom of a styrene tray. Discard one of the small triangles and snip the end off of one of the other small triangles. Cut notches where the two heavy lines are drawn in the diagram. Use the notches to attach the tail (the smaller piece that is now a quadrilateral) to the wing (the large triangle). Make adjustments as necessary to get your plane to fly.

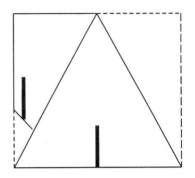

### 2. Distance

When you have your model flying well, take it to the test range and measure how far it can go. Try modifying your plane and retesting it, changing only one feature at a time. Record the changes and the new data. Try changing your plane at least once more.

### 3. Aerobatics

Make a cut in the tail to make a rudder and one cut in each wing to make ailerons. Experiment with bends in the rudder and flaps to see the effects on your model's flight patterns. (When bending the rudder and flaps, make small bends so the styrene doesn't break. If it does break, mend it with masking tape.)

### 4. Turns

Now devise a series of systematic experiments to find out exactly how bending the rudder and the ailerons will affect flight. Record your observations in your Toy Inventor's Log. Remember to change only one surface at a time. Use the information you learn to make your plane execute a smooth turn to one side.

### 5. Instructions

Get your plane to perform at least one maneuver, and then write instructions a child could follow to recreate the maneuver. When you have written the instructions, have another student read them to see if they work.

Inventing Toys ©2002 Zephyr Press, Tucson, Arizona • 800-232-2187 • www.zephyrpress.com

# Toy Inventor's Log—Toy Planes

**Project name** _____

**Team members** _____

| | |
|---|---|
| **Sketch**<br><br>Sketch how to make the plane.<br><br>Label the parts: wing, tail, ailerons, and rudder. | |
| **Data**<br><br>Record the longest flights you were able to achieve.<br><br>List the design changes that helped. | |

# Toy Inventor's Log—Toy Planes *(continued)*

| **Making Turns** | |
|---|---|
| What adjustments are needed to:<br><br>1. Fly up?<br><br>2. Fly down?<br><br>3. Roll the plane?<br><br>4. Turn smoothly to the left? | |

<br>

| When I bent the | The plane did |
|---|---|
| Ailerons up | |
| Ailerons down | |
| Rudder left | |
| Rudder right | |
| Left aileron up and right aileron down | |

| **Improvements**<br><br>List ideas for improving your toy. | |
|---|---|

| **Knowledge Gained**<br><br>List what you learned. | |
|---|---|

Signed: _____ Date: _____

Witness: _____

*Inventing Toys* ©2002 Zephyr Press, Tucson, Arizona • 800-232-2187 • www.zephyrpress.com

# Electric
## FANS

## Challenge

To build electric fans and to find uses for them

WORKSHOP

# Science Concepts

➤ *Electric Circuits*

➤ *Electric Motors*

➤ *Energy Storage and Transformations*

➤ *Measurement and Data Collection*

➤ *Experimental Design*

Students experiment with electric circuits to learn about a wide range of topics, including electric forces; chemical storage of energy; energy conversion from chemical storage to electricity to motion and heat; conductors and insulators; electric switches; and motors. When teams have created their fan inventions they can design experiments to test their effectiveness or longevity with a fixed source of energy (batteries).

### SAFETY NOTE

Students should use only direct current supplied by batteries for this workshop. At no point should they use or attempt to use alternating current from electrical outlets.

# Standards

| American Association for the Advancement of Science Benchmarks ||
| Chapter | Section |
|---|---|
| The Nature of Science | The Scientific World View<br>Scientific Inquiry<br>The Scientific Enterprise |
| The Nature of Technology | Technology and Science<br>Design and Systems<br>Issues in Technology |
| The Physical Setting | Energy Transformations<br>Motion<br>Forces of Nature |
| The Designed World | Energy Sources and Use |
| Common Themes | Systems |
| Habits of the Mind | Computation and Estimation<br>Manipulation and Observation<br>Communication Skills<br>Critical-Response Skills |

| National Research Council Science Education Standards ||
| Content Area | Abilities/Understanding |
|---|---|
| Science as Inquiry—Standard A | Abilities necessary to do scientific inquiry**<br>Understanding about scientific inquiry** |
| Physical Science—Standard B | Properties of objects and materials**<br>Position and motion of objects<br>Light, heat, electricity, and magnetism<br>Motions and forces*<br>Transfer of energy* |
| Science and Technology—Standard E | Abilities of technological design**<br>Understanding about science and technology** |
| History and Nature of Science | Science as a human endeavor**<br>Nature of science* |

** denotes standards apply for both K–4 and grades 5–8
* denotes standards for grades 5–8
No mark refers to standards for K–4.

# A Brief History of Fans

People have used fans since at least 3,000 BC. Both the Chinese and the Egyptians invented versions of fans. In Egypt, slaves supplied the energy that kept the fans moving to cool the privileged. In China, fan usage wasn't restricted to the rich and powerful; people fanned themselves. The Chinese transformed what might have been a mundane tool into a work of art. They introduced fans to the Japanese, who created their own version, the folding fan.

Industrial propeller fans were first employed in France starting in 1858 to ventilate mines. These may have been steam powered; we know they weren't electric. The electric fan was invented in 1891, years after the first electric motor was discovered by Michael Faraday (1821) and developed into a working model by Thomas Davenport (1837). Until electric batteries were developed (1859) and until homes had electricity (Edison started offering electric power in London in 1881 and in New York City the following year), there was no source of electric power for machines. Once electricity was available, a swarm of electrical inventions were created. Electric fans were one of these inventions.

# Materials

✔ *1.5–3.0 volt DC electric motors*

✔ *Alligator clip leads*

✔ *Masking tape*

✔ *D cell batteries*

✔ *Styrene food trays*

✔ *Insulated wire*

✔ *A wire stripper*

✔ *Scissors*

✔ *Propellers*

✔ *A candle and matches*

✔ *Paper clips, pencil lead, paper*

✔ *Aluminum foil*

✔ *Glue*

✔ *Optional: flashlight bulbs, mechanical pencil leads*

## NOTES

You can purchase the electrical supplies at an electronics store or through an electronics or science supply catalog (see the resources list on page 102). If possible, purchase motors that have wire leads soldered in place (they cost about $1.00 each). You will need one motor, a few alligator clips, and one or two D batteries per team. Have on hand at least one roll of insulated wire. In advance, prepare an ample supply of 12-inch pieces with stripped ends.

The styrene food trays provide a surface for anchoring the motor, wires, and switches. You could substitute cardboard or Masonite boards for the styrene.

You can purchase plastic propellers in hobby stores, over the Internet, or through catalogs. You need one per team and will want the least expensive ones you can find. Ideally the propellers will fit snugly onto the shafts of the motors, but if they don't you can make them. One way is to place a section of a cocktail straw onto the motor shaft. The straw should fit snugly on the shaft and will provide a slightly larger surface for attaching the propeller. If the propeller hole is still larger than the straw-covered shaft, carefully wrap an inch of clear tape around the straw or around the shaft. An alternative solution is to sharpen one end of a 1/4" dowel in a pencil sharpener and then cut off the sharpened end so the piece is about 1 inch long. Holding the flat end up in a vise, drill a hole that the motor shaft can fit into. Put a drop of glue on the sharp end and jam it into the opening in the propeller.

## NOTE

You can also show students how to make propellers out of aluminum foil. First cut a piece of foil about 2 inches long and 1 inch wide. Fold the foil in half twice, first lengthwise and then the other way, to give a stiffer propeller. Add small pieces of tape to strengthen the arms if desired. Find the center by balancing the folded strip on a pencil, and poke a hole through the foil there. Run the motor shaft into the hole and glue it in place. Finally, twist the ends of the aluminum propeller to get the desired pitch. Once students learn this method, they can experiment with different-sized propellers.

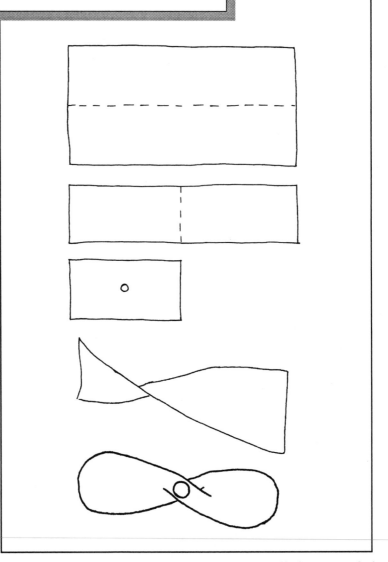

**Propellers can be made from folded and twisted aluminum foil.**

# Using Volunteers

Volunteers can prepare pieces of wire by cutting lengths of about a foot and stripping an inch of insulation off each end. They can also support teams as they experiment with circuits.

# Issuing the Challenge

Use the following script or your own words.

"Our toy company has purchased another company that makes small, direct-current motors. To boost sales of this new division, management has directed us to come up with new ideas for toys or toy-appliances using these motors.

"Today we want to focus on applications like fans, windmills, or toy hair dryers. Each team will get one electric motor, a battery, and a propeller. Your challenge is to design something that uses an electric motor. We'll all start by making simple motor-driven fans. Once you have a basic model operating, you can try different things to improve it. Come to me to show me your improved design and to ask for additional materials if you need them. Obviously we don't have all the materials that every project will require, so you will have to be creative. When you have built your invention you need to decide how to evaluate it and test it.

"We will use an objective rating scale to evaluate the fans so the Toy Company can decide which units to put into production. As part of the evaluation process, we will test the fans to see how much air they can move."

# Warm-Up

The day before the workshop ask students to take apart a flashlight at home to figure out how it works. Challenge them to identify the major three or four components and to diagram the circuit showing the bulb, switch, batteries, and conductors. In class, review basic electricity concepts and vocabulary by discussing how the flashlight works.

# Procedure

1. **Pair students up in teams and distribute basic materials to each team.**

   Start with one motor, one battery, and two alligator clip leads per team. They can request additional materials later if they develop a design that requires them.

2. **Allow students to get the motors working.**

   You can show them how to hook up the battery, or let them figure it out on their own.

3. **Distribute propellers.**

   Have students attach the propellers and play with these basic fans for a little while.

4. **Distribute the Fan Rating Criteria handout and Toy Inventor's Logs, and have students work on their fans.**

   Both handouts are supplied at the end of the notes for this workshop.

   Students who have limited experience with basic electrical concepts and devices may need considerable guidance. For example, they may not know that they can switch the lead wires to reverse the flow of air, or that they can make switches out of aluminum foil, paper clips, or other materials found in the classroom. On the other hand, some students will have many ideas for improving their inventions and will come to you on their own for additional materials.

The Fan Rating Criteria handout uses a fan's capacity to extinguish a candle from a distance as a measure of effectiveness, but if you choose not to use an open flame for testing fans, use paper strips instead. Cut out strips one-half inch wide and about five inches long and tape them to a yardstick suspended above a table. Create a way to measure the angle of deflection of the paper strips when a fan is blowing. Measure and record the greatest distance at which the fan deflects the paper strips to a defined minimal angle.

To make a variable-speed fan, students will need to experiment with various insulators and conductors. The fan will run fast when attached directly to a battery with wires. Connecting it to two or more batteries will make it run even faster. To get slower speeds, students can connect an alligator clip lead to a pencil lead and complete the circuit by touching the pencil point with the battery terminal. Or they can connect the leads to different positions on a mechanical pencil lead.

Teams can also experiment with the design of propellers. They can make a propeller out of aluminum foil and test it by determining the greatest distance at which the motor-driven propeller can extinguish the candle. Once they have measured the range of this propeller, they can make another propeller that is longer, shorter, fatter, skinnier, or one that has more or fewer arms, and compare its range to that of the first.

Some students may have ideas for incorporating their fans into toys or for creating simple toys that use the motor. Encourage creativity and experimentation.

## Teachable Moments

### ELECTRICAL FORCES AND DEVICES

When students have connected the circuit and have the propeller blowing, ask them how they could change the direction of airflow. (They could reverse the wires connected to the battery; they could reverse the pitch on the propeller; or they could put the propeller backwards on the motor shaft.) Ask teams what is providing the energy to move the air. What stores the energy until we need to use it? What does an electric motor do? (It converts electrical energy into mechanical energy.)

# Wrap-Up

Bring designing and testing activities to a close and have students report on what design features worked best. Also have them tell what use their team would make of the fan (or just the motor) and what they would call their creation. If desired, have them turn in the Fan Rating Criteria sheet.

Use directed questioning to reinforce what students learned about electric circuits, guiding them to use appropriate vocabulary. For example, elicit that to get the motor to spin, the circuit had to be complete. That is, there had to be a conductor connecting one battery terminal to one motor terminal and another conductor connecting the other motor terminal to the other battery terminal.

If any students used a second battery, have them share the details. How was it connected to the circuit? What effect did it have? Discuss the fact that for direct current motors (but not for alternating current motors), higher voltage makes motors spin faster (to a certain point). Ask whether anyone was successful in changing the voltage and the speed of the motor by using different conductors. What materials conducted electricity well and what materials didn't?

If they haven't already done so, have students make notes of what they learned in their Toy Inventor's Logs.

# Follow-Up Activities

1. Demonstrate how to generate electricity by using a room fan or a shop vac to blow on one of the student-made fans. Hook up a small digital voltmeter (available for about $10) to the motor (disconnected from the battery). Slowly bring the room fan or blower close to the blades to get them spinning, and have students watch the voltage on the voltmeter. Then switch the voltmeter leads to change the direction of flow of electricity. Discuss how electric motors transform energy between mechanical forms and electric forms and can operate in either direction (mechanical into electrical as an electric generator, or electrical into mechanical as an electric motor).

2. Challenge students to make a light for a child's toy box, such that when the box lid is opened, the light will come on. They can use a shoebox for the toy box. The challenge will be to make a switch that is off when the lid is closed and on when the lid is opened.

3. If any students are especially excited about the electrical experiments, suggest they research Philo Farnsworth. Growing up in Rigby, Idaho, Farnsworth had few of the advantages of his peers living in metropolitan areas. However one of his high school teachers saw the spark of genius in Philo and took the time to work with him in his electrical experiments. We remember Philo today as a principal inventor of the television. (Try out some of the projects in the recommended books below and watch for the next Philo Farnsworth to appear in your classroom!)

# Extensions to Other Subjects

Students may be amazed that the famous and prolific Thomas Edison was on the losing side of one of the great technological debates. In the early days of electrical power, Edison favored direct current over alternating current, and he fought intensely to convince the public that alternating current was too dangerous to have in their homes. Have students research his famous battle with Tesla (*Young Inventors at Work* by Sobey provides a short summary). Or they can study various aspects of life in America before and after the dawn of the electric age to learn what the impacts of this technology were.

# Resources

## Books

***Blinkers and Buzzers*** (Bernie Zubrowski). Describes fun electrical projects made from inexpensive components.

***Experimenting with Electricity and Magnetism*** (Ovid Wong). Covers a spectrum of experiments for kids.

***Put a Fan in Your Hat*** (Robert Carrow). Suggests zany, fun projects using electricity and magnetism.

***Science Projects About Electricity and Magnetism*** (Robert Gardner). Covers a broad spectrum of experiments.

***The Way Things Work*** (David Macaulay). Shows the internal workings of batteries.

***Young Inventors at Work! Learning Science by Doing Science*** (Ed Sobey). Includes two dozen short stories on inventors and inventions.

## Sources for Electrical Supplies

### Kelvin

www.kelvin.com
(800) KELVIN-W (535-8469)
Has a good assortment of technology
supplies for education.

### Jameco

www.jameco.com
(800) 831-4242
Puts out an electronics components and
computer products catalog.

### The Science Source

www.thesciencesource.com
(800) 299-5469
Sells materials for design technology and
science projects.

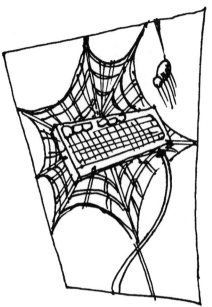

Name _____

# Fan Rating Criteria

To aid its quest for the perfect fan, The Toy Factory has established the following evaluation criteria. How does your fan rate?

| Criteria | Possible Rating Points | Your Fan |
|---|---|---|
| Fan has an on-off switch | 10 | _____ |
| Fan can reverse directions without reversing the propeller | 5 | _____ |
| Fan can extinguish a candle: | | |
|     From 24 inches away | 25 | _____ |
|     From 18 inches away | 20 | _____ |
|     From 12 inches away | 10 | _____ |
|     From 6 inches away | 5 | _____ |
| Fan can operate at variable speeds | 15 | |
| Fan has a great name, unique design, and creative use | 10 | _____ |

**Total rating points for your fan**             _____

See if you can improve your score by changing your invention.

# Toy Inventor's Log—Electric Fans

**Project name** _____

**Team members** _____

| | |
|---|---|
| **Use**<br><br>Write how you would use the fan or the electric motor in a toy. | |
| **Name**<br><br>Give a name to the toy you are making. | |
| **Diagram**<br><br>Sketch the electric circuit you created.<br><br>Show the energy source, electric motors, switches, and wires. | |

| | |
|---|---|
| **Testing Data**<br><br>How did you test your invention and what did you learn from the tests?<br><br>How could you improve the design? | |
| **Knowledge Gained**<br><br>List what you learned that will help you with inventing your next toy. | |

Signed: _____   Date: _____

Witness: _____

# Part III
# Additional Activities and Resources

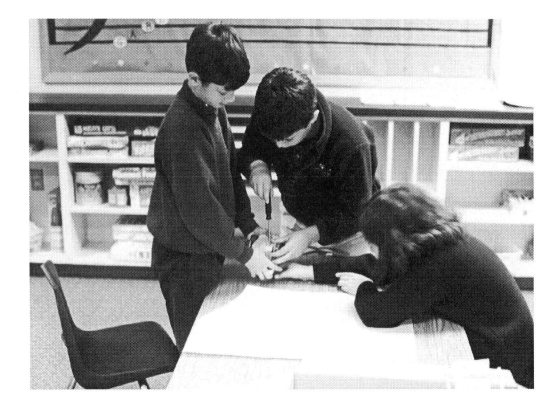

*Learning science is something students do, not something that is done to them.*

—National Research Council, National Science Education Standards

# Reverse ENGINEERING

## Adapted for Use with Push 'n Go Cars

## Challenge

To experiment in order to test conjectures about internal mechanisms of toys, and then to confirm the findings by taking the toys apart

**WORKSHOP (ADAPTED)**

# Science Concepts

➤ *Energy Storage*

➤ *Energy Conversion*

➤ *Friction*

➤ *Gears*

➤ *Experimental Design*

➤ *Data Collection and Analysis*

Inventors take things apart to find out how they work. In this activity, students work in teams of two to operate a toy car, think about how it works, and then take it apart to see if their ideas are correct. Reverse engineering gives them good experience in experimental design, thus setting the stage for other workshops in which they will build their own toys and test them.

This activity is a logical setting for introducing concepts and vocabulary related to forces and energy. The toy car that students will be investigating uses a simple spring-based mechanism to operate. The toy user inputs energy into the toy. The energy is stored in the spring, which is released to make the toy work. The car also uses a set of gears, which provides an additional avenue for exploration.

Although sound is not the main topic students will be exploring, the toys do make noise. You could challenge students to think how the sound is generated and dissipated during this activity.

# Standards

| American Association for the Advancement of Science Benchmarks | |
|---|---|
| **Chapter** | **Section** |
| The Nature of Science | The Scientific World View<br>Scientific Inquiry<br>The Scientific Enterprise |
| The Nature of Mathematics | Mathematics, Science, and Technology |
| The Nature of Technology | Technology and Science<br>Design and Systems<br>Issues in Technology |
| The Physical Setting | Energy Transformations<br>Motion |
| The Designed World | Energy Sources and Use |
| Common Themes | Systems<br>Models |
| Habits of the Mind | Values and Attitudes<br>Computation and Estimation<br>Manipulation and Observation<br>Communication Skills<br>Critical-Response Skills |

| National Research Council Science Education Standards | |
|---|---|
| **Content Area** | **Abilities/Understanding** |
| Science as Inquiry—Standard A | Abilities necessary to do scientific inquiry**<br>Understanding about scientific inquiry** |
| Physical Science—Standard B | Properties of objects and materials**<br>Position and motion of objects<br>Motions and forces*<br>Transfer of energy* |
| Science and Technology—Standard E | Abilities of technological design**<br>Understanding about science and technology** |
| Science in Personal and Social Perspectives—Standard F | Science and technology in local challenges<br>Science and technology in society* |
| History and Nature of Science | Science as a human endeavor**<br>Nature of science* |

** denotes standards apply for both K–4 and grades 5–8
* denotes standards for grades 5–8
No mark refers to standards for K–4.

# A Brief History of Springs

See page 21.

# Materials

- ✔ *Push 'n Go™ cars*
- ✔ *Phillips screwdrivers*
- ✔ *Safety goggles*
- ✔ *Measuring sticks or tapes*

## NOTES

Push 'n Go cars are made by Tomy® and are available from large chain retail toy stores for several dollars each. You will need to provide one toy car per team of students. Although Push 'n Go cars cost more than pullback cars, they can be reassembled so you can use them again.

Since teams will all be using Phillips screwdrivers at the same time, it is desirable if you can provide a screwdriver for each team. Be sure that the ones you provide are able to reach and turn the screws on this toy. The Phillips screws involved are relatively large and the screwdriver needs to have a long shaft to reach them.

The goggles are a safety measure. Although the spring in this toy is unlikely to fly out, students should protect their eyes when they are disassembling the car.

## Using Volunteers

Volunteers can help teams collect data and use tools. If they are not experienced with this type of learning process, you will want to orient them before the activity. In particular, remind them not to take over from the students in an attempt to help teams "get it right." Getting it wrong is often the best way to learn (as long as no damage or injuries occur) and students need to have the opportunity to try their ideas and assess whether their understandings were accurate or not.

## Issuing the Challenge

Use the following script or your own words.

"You may be surprised to hear this, but we've suddenly all changed jobs. This place is no longer a school, it's a toy company! My new job is manager of product development, and I've hired all of you talented inventors as design engineers. The company president [insert name of school principal if desired] has issued a challenge for us today.

"It seems that one of our competitors has a toy car that is selling extremely well, and we may be interested in making and selling a toy like it. We need to understand how their cars work, how we could make something similar, and what we could change to make our version sell better.

"What we want to do today is to try out the cars, predict what makes them go, and then take them apart to confirm our analysis. Later we can try to come up with new designs for the toys."

# Warm-Up

Hold up and then demonstrate a Push 'n Go car. Elicit conjectures as to how the toy works, and summarize them on the board. Include ideas whether they are right or wrong. These ideas can serve as hypotheses for students to test.

## Teachable Moments

### ENERGY AND VELOCITY

While students are operating the cars, ask directed questions to stimulate thinking about relevant concepts of physics. For example, ask students if the toys need energy to move. Where does the energy come from? After someone transfers energy to the toy, it is stored internally. How is the energy stored? After it is released, why does the toy eventually stop? Where did the energy go? Does the toy travel at the same speed through a run? Or did it start slowly, build up speed, and slow down? As students answer the questions in their own words, coach them to substitute appropriate vocabulary. For example, "Acceleration is what we call changes in velocity."

# Procedure

1. **Pair students up in teams and distribute Push 'n Go cars.**

   Allow students to play with the toys for a few minutes to experience how the cars work. Tell them to think about what the inside of the car might look like and what might be happening to make the cars move.

2. **Distribute the Experimental Design handout and Toy Inventor's Log.**

   The Experimental Design handout is supplied at the end of the notes for this workshop. The Toy Inventor's Log is on pages 29–30. As directed by the handout, students will be thinking further about the inside of the car, and measuring the distance the car goes on one full push. They will use their logs to record their ideas.

3. **Ask students to devise and run an experiment to test their ideas about how the cars work.**

   Students may not be able to figure out how the vertical motion is transformed into horizontal motion, but challenge them to think about it. If they have trouble figuring out what device stores energy in the toy, have them depress the character while you ask them what is resisting their pressing. Ask them what type of device pushes back when you push on it.

4. **Distribute Phillips screwdrivers and safety goggles and have teams disassemble the cars, then study and manipulate the internal mechanism.**

   The handout directs them to explore the gear mechanism. The large gears have 22 teeth and the small gears have 10. So the gear ratio is 2.2:1 for each of the three pairs of gears. Each time the first gear (the one contacting the piece that

## Teachable Moments

### CONJECTURING

Generating a hypothesis about a hidden internal mechanism is difficult, and students may need some help. Ask the class to describe how the toy operates. Does the distance the car travels depend on how far they push down? Does the distance the car travels *equal* the distance they push? Students should be able to recognize that since they push down a few inches to get the car to move forward several feet, there must be a mechanism in the car that multiplies the distance it can travel.

moves up and down) makes one rotation, the axle will turn 10.65 times (2.2 x 2.2 x 2.2). The drive wheels have a diameter of approximately 1⅝ inches, which gives a circumference of 5.11 inches. Thus for one complete rotation of the first gear, the drive wheels will travel 54.37 inches. In comparing this distance to the measurement of how far the toy travels, remember that the car continues to roll even after the spring has fully extended itself. That is, momentum carries the car forward. Also, we don't know (and can't tell) how many times the first gear turns while the spring is unwinding.

5. **Have teams reassemble their cars.**

   Give students time afterwards to document their workshop experience by writing in their Inventor's Logs.

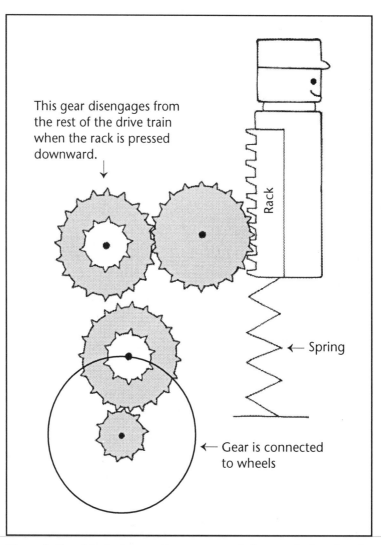

**The relationship between the gears and the vertical spring in a Push 'n Go car**

## Teachable Moments

### GEARS AND MOTION

After students have observed the gear mechanism and answered the questions on the handout, reinforce their learning by asking directed questions. For example, "What do the gears do? What happens when a big gear pushes a little gear? Do the gears speed up or slow down the motion of the drive mechanism? How does the up-and-down motion in the Push 'n Go car change to the circular motion of the wheels?"

# Wrap-Up

After checking to make sure all the cars have been reassembled properly, bring the toy car activity to a close and have students report on their experiences. Emphasize the experimental nature of the workshop, reminding them that they first made hypotheses about how the cars worked, then tried to verify those hypotheses by observing how the intact cars operated, and finally used "reverse engineering" to confirm their results by taking apart the cars.

# Follow-Up Activities

1. Have teams make their Push 'n Go toys travel in a curved path by wrapping rubber bands around one of the rear wheels. Can they have it turn around completely in one run?

2. Have students determine the relationship between the vertical distance the character is depressed and the horizontal distance the Push 'n Go toy travels. They can collect data, graph the data, and determine the slope of the line that best fits the data.

3. Have students test the cars on different surfaces to learn about friction. For example, if they used the cars on a wooden or concrete floor earlier, have them try with carpet. On what surface does the car travel farthest? Why?

4. Ask students to describe other machines in which the direction of motion changes between the driving force (or motor) and the wheels. They may know, for example, that in most cars the up-and-down motion of the pistons is transformed to a rotational motion that is perpendicular to the motion of the wheels.

5. Have students generate a list of toys that use stored energy and tell how the energy is stored. Discuss types of storage mechanisms, such as batteries (chemical), rubber bands or springs (mechanical), and elevation (gravitational).

6. Hand out the Energy Storage Word Search Puzzle (see page 31) and challenge students to find all 21 things that store energy. See Appendix for answers.

# Extensions to Other Subjects

1. Assign students to write the script for a one-minute television commercial promoting Push 'n Go cars. Then have them read or act out the commercial for the class.

2. For an art project, have students create covers for their Toy Inventor's Logs. They could illustrate them with drawings of the Push 'n Go car (or its inner parts) or with other art related to science concepts or inventing.

# Resources

***The Way Things Work*** (David Macaulay). Shows how many devices work and gives illustrations of several types of springs.

***Young Inventors at Work! Learning Science by Doing Science*** (Ed Sobey). Lists several other activities for reverse engineering.

***Teaching Physics with Toys*** (Beverley Taylor et al.). Suggests several other experiments to run using Push 'n Go toys.

# Reverse Engineering—Push 'n Go™ Cars

## Experimental Design

How do you think this toy works? Make a *hypothesis*. See if you can verify your hypothesis by experimenting. Then take the car apart to check.

1. **Think about some basic questions.**

   How does the toy change the direction of force? (You push *down* on the character to get the toy to move, but the toy moves *forward*.)

   What device stores energy in the toy?

   Does the car travel farther when you push the character down farther?

   How far does the car travel when you depress the character fully? Measure the distance.

2. **Run an experiment to learn more about how the car works.**

   Start with a hypothesis. Write it in your Inventor's Log.

   Create an experiment to investigate whether your hypothesis is true.

   Record your results in your Inventor's Log.

3. **Take apart your car.**

   Remove the four screws that hold the toy together. Observe the parts inside. Were you correct about how the toy works?

   Sketch the mechanism in your Toy Inventor's Log.

   Count the number of teeth on the large and small gears. (Mark one tooth with a pencil and carefully rotate the gear so you can count, stopping at the last tooth before the one you marked.) When a large-diameter gear meshes with a smaller gear, the speed of rotation increases. It increases according to the ratio of the number of teeth. Calculate the ratio of the number of teeth from the large gear to the small.

   Find out how many times the axle turns for every turn of the first gear. You can calculate this or observe it.

   Figure out how far the car will travel for each rotation of the first gear. (You will need to measure the diameter of the wheels to calculate this.) Is it the same as the distance measurement you made before you took the car apart? Can you explain why or why not?

# Five Additional Toy Inventing Activities (Outlines)

Listed below are outlines for additional toy inventing activities.
You will find complete details in the reference material.

| Toys | Materials | Procedure | References |
|---|---|---|---|
| **Flying Disks** | Paper plates<br>Metal washers<br>Masking tape<br>Scissors | Students make Frisbees™ out of paper plates by cutting and bending paper plates and by adding weight to the outside rim. The goal is to get them to fly the farthest | *Fantastic Flying Fun with Science* (Ed Sobey) |
| **Tops** | Dowels, wooden wheels or paper plates, and washers Alternatively, CDs plus long bolts, washers, and nuts | Students make tops and try to get them to spin as long as possible | *Young Inventors at Work!* (Ed Sobey) and *Tops* (Bernie Zubrowski) |
| **Musical Instruments** | Wide assortment of common materials including rubber bands, string, cans, straws, paper, milk cartons, and paper clips | Students make wind, string, and percussion instruments from common materials and then play a song | *Rubber-Band Banjos and Java Jive Bass* (Alex Sabbeth), *Make Mine Music!* (Tom Walther), and *Sound Designs— A Handbook of Musical Instrument Building* (Reinhold Banek and Jon Scoville) |
| **Lunch Boxes** | Aluminum foil<br>Paper<br>Cardboard<br>Masking tape<br>Styrene<br>Masking tape | Students design and build lunch boxes that insulate. The challenge is to keep an ice cube from melting for as long as possible. | |
| **Catapults** | Rubber bands<br>Rulers<br>Dried peas<br>Blocks of wood<br>Plastic spoons | Students construct catapults to launch a dried pea or bean as far as possible | *Young Inventors at Work!* (Ed Sobey) |

# Resources _____

## Other Creativity-Based Learning Programs

You can tap into other curriculum and ideas for creativity-based learning activities through the organizations listed below.

**Destination Imagination**
>Promotes creative problem solving through an annual competition at the local, regional, state, and world levels. They offer nearly a dozen problems each year and several are based in technology. Contact them or get information through their website at www.destinationimagination.org.

**Kids Invent Toys**
>This group offers one-week summer camps, after-school programs, and in-school inventing programs. Visit their website at www.kidsinvent.org.

**National Science Teachers Association**
>The NSTA promotes and runs invention competitions for several companies. To get information, go to their website at www.nsta.org/ programs.

**Odyssey of the Mind**
>A parallel organization to Destination Imagination. Most states have either Destination Imagination or Odyssey of the Mind. Visit their website at www.odysseyofthemind.com.

**Science Olympiad**
>An annual science competition that includes some projects requiring creativity and inventiveness. Visit their website at www.geocities.com/ CapeCanaveral/Lab/9699.

# Books, Magazines, and Websites
## Books

This following list includes books on inventing, science and science learning, the history of technology, and why people strive to make creative and inventive works.

American Association for the Advancement of Science. 1993. *Benchmarks for Science Literacy.* New York: Oxford University Press.

Baker, R. 1976. New and Improved . . . *Inventors and Inventions that Have Changed the Modern World.* London: British Museum Publications, Ltd. A great resource, listing inventions and their patent numbers and inventors.

Baldwin, Neil. 1995. *Edison.* New York: Hyperion. One of the best of the many biographies.

Banek, Reinhold and Jon Scoville. 1995. *Sound Designs. A Handbook of Musical Instrument Building.* Berkeley, Calif.: Ten Speed Press.

Bunch, Bryan, and Alexander Hellemans. *The Timetables of Technology.* 1993. New York: Simon & Schuster. A great resource for finding the origins of technology.

Carrow, Robert. 1997. *Put a Fan in Your Hat!* New York: McGraw-Hill. Provides a variety of electrical contraptions for kids to make and invent.

Castro, Elizabeth. 1996. *HTML for the World Wide Web.* Berkeley, Calif.: Peachpit Press.

Churchill, E. Richard. 1990. *Fantastic Flying Paper Toys.* New York: Sterling.

Csikszentmihalyi, Mihaly. 1990. *Flow: The Psychology of Optimal Experience.* New York: Harper Perennial. To understand "flow" is to understand how to get kids to learn.

———. 1997. *Creativity: Flow and the Psychology of Discovery and Invention.* New York: Harper Perennial. Addresses the question of what makes people in creative pursuits work so hard.

Davis, Meredith, Peter Hawley, Bernard McMullan, and Gertrude Spilka. 1997. *Design as a Catalyst for Learning.* Alexandria, Va.: Association for Supervision and Curriculum Development.

DeMatteis, Bob. 1999. *From Patent to Profit.* New York: Penguin Putnam. Good advice on how to take a creative idea to market.

Design as a Catalyst for Learning. 1997. Alexandria, Va.: Association for Supervision and Curriculum Development.

Dryden, Gordon, and Jeannette Vos. 1994. *The Learning Revolution.* Rolling Hills Estates, Calif.: Jalmar Press.

Eichelberger, Barbara, and Connie Larson. 1993. *Constructions for Children.* White Plains, N.Y.: Dale Seymour Publications. A variety of fun projects for younger kids.

Epstein, Robert. 1995. *Creativity Games for Trainers.* New York: McGraw-Hill.

Francis, Neil. 1988. *Super Flyers.* Reading, Mass.: Addison-Wesley Publishing Company, Inc. Flying models kids can make.

Friedhoffer, Fred. 1995. *Toying Around with Science.* Danbury, Ct.: Franklin Watts. The physics behind toys and gags.

Gardner, Howard. 1983. *Frames of Mind.* New York: Basic Books.

————. 1993. *The Unschooled Mind: How Children Think and How Schools Should Teach.* New York: Basic Books.

Gardner, Robert. 1994. *Science Projects About Electricity and Magnetism.* Berkeley Heights, N.J.: Enslow.

Hawke, David Freeman. 1998. *Nuts and Bolts from the Past.* New York: Harper & Row. History of American technology, 1776-1860.

Hayden, Robert. 1988. *Eight Black American Inventors.* Reading, Mass.: Addison-Wesley.

Hindle, Brooke, and Steven Lubar. 1988. *Engines of Change.* Washington, D.C.: Smithsonian Institution Press. The American Industrial Revolution, 1790-1860.

Hoffman, David. 1996. *Kid Stuff.* San Francisco, Calif.: Chronicle Books. Background on those favorite toys of the baby boomers.

Hughes, Thomas P. 1989. *American Genesis.* New York: Viking Penguin. The history of technology in America.

*Inventive Genius.* 1991. New York: Time-Life Books. Great stories behind inventions.

Karwatka, Dennis. 1996. *Technology's Past. America's Industrial Revolution and the People Who Delivered the Goods.* Ann Arbor, Mich.: Prakken Publications.

Macaulay, David. 1988. *The Way Things Work.* Boston, Mass.: Houghton Mifflin. A must-have reference book.

Macdonald, Anne L. 1992. *Feminine Ingenuity. Women and Invention in America.* New York: Ballantine. The most authoritative book on women inventors in America.

McBride, Carol. 2000. *Making Magnificent Machines: Fun with Math, Science, and Engineering.* Tucson, Ariz.: Zephyr Press.

Miller, Lucy. 1998. *KidTech. Hands-On Problem Solving with Design Technology for Grades 5–8.* Parsippany, N.J.: Dale Seymour. Ideas for projects and skill-building activities.

National Research Council. 1996. *National Science Education Standards.* Washington, D.C.: National Academy of Sciences.

Panati, Charles. 1987. *Extraordinary Origins of Everyday Things.* New York: Harper Trade. A great reference for finding out where things come from.

Pfiffner, George. 1994. *Earth-Friendly Toys.* New York: John Wiley. Making toys and games from recyclable materials.

Rohnke, Karl. 1989. *Cowstails and Cobras II. A Guide to Games, Initiatives, Ropes Courses, and Adventure Curriculum.* Dubuque, Iowa: Kendall/Hunt.

Ruhe, Benjamin, and Eric Darnell. 1985. *Boomerang. How to Throw, Catch, and Make It.* New York: Workman Publishing.

Sabbeth, Alex. 1997. *Rubber-Band Banjos and a Java Jive Bass.* New York: John Wiley.

Sobey, Ed. 1996. *Inventing Stuff.* Parsippany, N.J.: Dale Seymour Publications. Provides background on the inventing process for kids with information on brainstorming, making mockups, and what to do with completed inventions.

———. 1996. *Wrapper Rockets and Trombone Straws.* New York: McGraw-Hill. Shows science-learning activities you can do at restaurants, including the straw flute.

———. 1997. *Car Smarts: Activities for the Open Road.* New York: McGraw-Hill. Activities and fun science for long road trips.

———. 1998. *Just Plane Smart.* New York: McGraw-Hill. Everything you want to know about the science and history of flying in planes, along with fun puzzles and activities.

———. 1999. *Young Inventors at Work—Learning Science by Doing Science.* Glenview, Ill.: Good Year Books. Activities for design technology and a series of original stories about inventors and inventions.

———. 1999. *How to Enter and Win an Invention Contest.* Berkeley Heights, N.J.: Enslow Publishing. How to find and enter invention contests for students, and how to invent a new product, process, or material for contests.

———. 2000. *Fantastic Flying Fun with Science.* New York: McGraw-Hill. Demonstrations to conduct and flying models to make.

————. 2000. *Reel Science: Science of the Entertainment Industry.* New York: Franklin Watts. Activities and explanation of how technology works in movies, TV, videotapes, and computer games.

————. 2000. *Wacky Water Fun with Science.* New York: McGraw-Hill. Demonstrations with water, and floating and sinking models to build.

————. 2002. *Blow Up This Book.* New York: Franklin Watts. Describes safe explosions to explore and other "blow ups."

Taylor, Beverley A. P., James Poth, and Dwight J. Portman. 1995. *Teaching Physics with Toys.* New York: Learning Triangle Press. Activities for K–9.

Tennekes, Hank. 1996. *The Simple Science of Flight.* Cambridge, Mass.: MIT Press.

Thimmesh, Catherine. 2000. *Girls Think of Everything: Stories of Ingenious Inventions by Women.* Boston, Mass.: Houghton Mifflin. The story of how women throughout the ages have invented items in response to the situations of everyday life.

Thompson, Charles "Chic". 1994. *What a Great Idea!* New York: Harper Trade.

U.S. Department of Labor. 1991. *What Work Requires of Schools: A SCANS Report for America 2000.* Washington, D.C.

Walker, Jearl. 1977. *The Flying Circus of Physics with Answers.* New York: John Wiley and Sons.

Walther, Tom. 1981. *Make Mine Music!* New York: Little, Brown.

Wong, Ovid K. 1993. *Experimenting with Electricity and Magnetism.* New York: Franklin Watts.

Wood, Elizabeth A. 1968. *Science from Your Airplane Window.* New York: Dover.

Zubrowski, Bernie. 1989. *Tops. Building and Experimenting with Spinning Toys.* New York: Morrow/Avon.

————. 1991. *Blinkers and Buzzers.* New York: Morrow/Avon.

## Magazines

*American Heritage of Invention and Technology.* A great quarterly magazine on the history of inventions and technology. Use these stories to weave history and science together.

*Inventor's Digest.* A magazine for professional inventors.
Website: www.inventorsdigest.com

## Websites

www.kidsinvent.org
> Kids Invent Toys site, featuring web pages made by kids to communicate about their inventions.

www.invent.org
> Inventure Place, home of the National Inventors Hall of Fame. Includes biographies for the dozens on inventors in the Hall of Fame.

http://web.mit.edu/invent/www/archive.html
> Inventor archives of the Lemelson-MIT's Program Invention Dimension. Has biographies of inventors and background on inventions.

www.acgilbert.org
> A. C. Gilbert's Discovery Village, home of the National Toy Hall of Fame. Check it out to see what toys are in the Hall. Nominate your favorite if it isn't in already.

www.patentcafe.com
> A resource for inventors, teachers, and students. Links to a variety of inventing sites.

www.InventorsDigest.com
> *Inventor's Digest* Magazine.

www.inventored.org
> Ron Riley's education page with resources for kids.

www.howstuffworks.com
> Descriptions and illustrations of how a variety of devices work.

http://erwin.phys.virginia.edu/Education/Teaching/HowThingsWork/
> Shows how various devices operate.

http://www.vrd.org/locator/subject.html
> Links to "Ask an expert" pages.

www.nsta.org
> NSTA site. Lists Duracell and other inventing competitions run by the NSTA.

www.letu.edu/community/invention/
> An invention contest conducted by LeTourneau University in Texas.

www.sbgschool.com/teacher_activities/convention/index.html
> The Invention Convention.

www.htmlgoodies.com
> The place to look to find codes for writing HTML websites.

www.uspto.gov
> The U.S. Patent and Trademark Office site.

www.patents.ibm.com
> A great site for finding patents.

www.toy-tma.com
> Website of the Toy Manufacturers Association, the trade group representing U.S. toymakers.

www.newhorizons.org/ofc_nita.html
> National Inventive Thinking Association. Organization offers a quarterly newsletter with ideas on how to use inventing in the classroom, and conducts conferences.

www.docie.com
> A site dedicated to helping new inventors market their inventions.

# Appendix

Answers to Energy Storage Word Search Puzzle,
Workshop 1, page 31

across    down    diagonal

# Answers to Toy Cars Crossword Puzzle, Workshop 2, page 48

# Answers to Ships Word Search Puzzle, Workshop 3, page 62

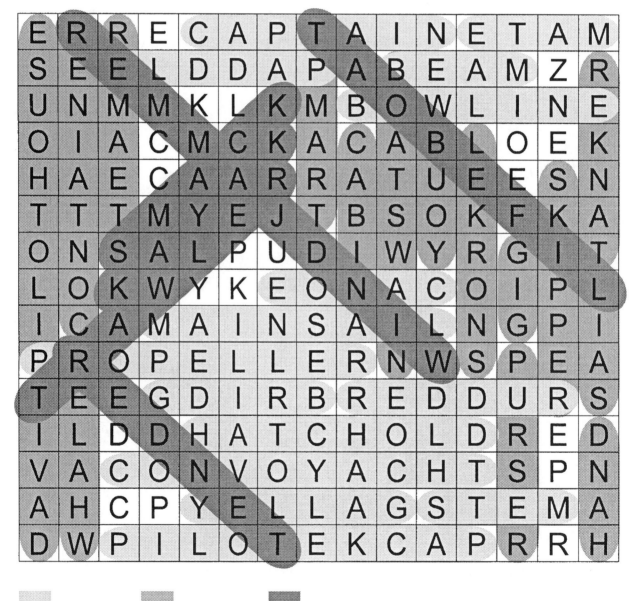

across    down    diagonal

# Index _____

# About the Author

After nearly 20 years directing museums, Ed Sobey created the Northwest Invention Center to serve schools and museums with hands-on programs and exhibits and to help inventors. Ed also originated and hosted a television show on inventing and co-hosted a science series for Ohio Public Broadcast Network. He holds a Ph.D. in oceanography from Oregon State University and teaches museum management at the University of Washington. Ed is the author of the popular titles, *Inventing Stuff* and *How to Win Invention Contests,* and more than 13 other books on subjects from backpacking to robots and kids' science projects.

# Learning—and Teaching—Is Fun
## *with These Resources from Zephyr Press*

## IMAGITRONICS
**Mind-Stretching Scenarios to Launch Creative Thought and Develop Problem-Solving Skills**
*Don Ambrose*

While traveling, you see a strange game being played in a stadium. Three teams of eight players each are chasing a large rubber ball on a triangular field . . . How is this game played? What are the rules? Draw several players in action.

Don Ambrose's delightful *Imagitronics* gives you and your students 71 unique and inventive scenarios to stimulate creative and critical thinking and artistic design. In the example above your students will imagine how this peculiar sport is played and may even set up a practice field to try out the game. These fantastic scenarios and quirky illustrations will enrich the minds of the brightest children and engage the interest of underachievers.

**1171-W . . . $29.95**
Grades 4–10
ISBN: 1-56976-141-8
160 pages

## CYBERTRIPS IN SOCIAL STUDIES
**Online Field Trips for All Ages**
*Scott Mandel*

*Cybertrips in Social Studies* takes you and your students on virtual field trips to far-away people and long-ago places and to the heart of incidents that shape our world, its history, and its cultures.

The interactive nature of the World Wide Web allows you and your students to *be there*—whether "there" is in an igloo at the Arctic circle or at Place de la Bastille in 18th century France. The 12 complete trips include community, history, and humanities field trips with various grade levels. Web savvy? These cybertrips are complete and ready to go. Don't know how to start? This step-by-step handbook teaches you how to create the trip, how to update the material, and how to adapt to the ever-changing resources available on the World Wide Web.

**1170-W . . . $26.95**
Grades K–12
ISBN: 1-56976-145-0
144 pages

## ART MATTERS
**Strategies, Ideas, and Activities to Strengthen Learning across the Curriculum**
*Eileen S. Prince*

Are you a history or math teacher looking to enrich your curriculum? Perhaps the art program at your school has been cut, and you've been asked to add art to your teaching schedule. Or, maybe you're the administrator who knows that **students who study the arts do better on such tests as the SAT.**

Award-winning teacher Eileen Prince brings you easy-to-use strategies and lesson plans to help you integrate art across the curriculum. The visual arts can be used to explore math, science, and history, and to cultivate critical-thinking skills. Art specialists will learn strategies for introducing many other subjects into their lesson plans.

> *"My artwork has also helped me in history. The artwork from the time really shows you how different people felt about different things . . . you feel closer to the people of the time."*
>
> —Alyssa, student

**1152-W . . . $27.95**
Grades K–12
ISBN: 1-56976-129-9
192 pages

## MAKING MAGNIFICENT MACHINES
**Fun with Math, Science, and Engineering**
*Carol McBride*

Students meet national science and math standards as they build cars that really race, a Ferris wheel that moves, ducks that lay golden eggs, and lots more amazing mechanical projects. You'll appreciate watching the enthusiasm of kids learning about abstract concepts like kinetic and potential energy, centrifugal force, and resistance. And they'll experiment with inclined planes, fulcrums, pulleys, and principles of flight. All 14 projects use easy-to-find recycled materials.

**1104-W . . . $24.95**
Grades K–8
ISBN: 1-56976-102-7
128 pages

*More than 100*

## BRAIN FOO

**Games That Mak
Kids Think**

*Paul Fleisher*

4/8/65

These games are all classroom-tested and tailored toward enhancing the intelligences of the children you teach. You'll find reproducible game boards and word, math, and strategy games. Games from faraway places like Africa, Denmark, New Zealand, and Indonesia will enhance your studies of other countries. These games are easy to use since most need little more than paper and pencil.

**1088-W . . . $29.95**
Grades 4–12+
ISBN: 1-56976-072-1
208 pages

## PORT TO LEARN

to Challenge
ntial Learners

gram to
e
ur high-
Give
port

at

Tickets for Success

projects in each of five content areas. Fasten your seatbelt, sit back, and assess learning through your students' original stories, speeches, and Internet-based projects. Your students will soar with pride in the frequent-flyer miles they earn with their *Passport to Learn*.

**1123-W . . . $27.95**
Grades 4–8
ISBN: 1-56976-125-6
192 pages

---

## Order Form

| Qty. | Item # | Title | Unit Price | Total |
|------|--------|-------|-----------|-------|
|      |        |       |           |       |
|      |        |       |           |       |
|      |        |       |           |       |
|      |        |       |           |       |

Name _____

Address _____

City _____

State _____ Zip _____

Phone (_____) _____

E-mail _____

**Method of payment (check one):**

❑ Check or Money Order  ❑ Visa

❑ MasterCard  ❑ Purchase Order Attached

Credit Card No. _____

Expires _____

Signature _____

| | |
|---|---|
| Subtotal | |
| Sales Tax (AZ residents, 5.6%) | |
| S & H (10% of subtotal–min $5.50) | |
| Total (U.S. funds only) | |

CANADA: add 30% for S & H and G.S.T.

☎

Please include your phone number in case we have questions about your order.

## Call, write, e-mail, or FAX for your FREE catalog!

## Zephyr Press

P.O. Box 66006-W
Tucson, AZ 85728-6006

1-800-232-2187
520-322-5090
FAX 520-323-9402
neways2learn@zephyrpress.com